I SAW
THE WELSH
REVIVAL

AMBASSADOR

BELFAST, NORTHERN IRELAND
GREENVILLE, SOUTH CAROLINA

I SAW
THE WELSH
REVIVAL

1904 ~ CENTENARY EDITION ~ 2004

BY
DAVID MATTHEWS

AMBASSADOR

BELFAST, NORTHERN IRELAND
GREENVILLE, SOUTH CAROLINA

I Saw The Welsh Revival

ISBN 1 84030 147 3

Published by the Ambassador Group
Ambassador Publications
a division of
Ambassador Productions Ltd.
Providence House
Ardenlee Street,
Belfast,
BT6 8QJ
Northern Ireland
www.ambassador-productions.com
&
Ambassador Emerald International
427 Wade Hampton Blvd.
Greenville
SC 29609, USA
www.emeraldhouse.com

PREFACE

Requests have been made, at various times, for an authoritative description of the marvelous effusion of the Holy Spirit which occurred in Wales during the years 1904-05, and shook the whole nation from center to circumference. It transformed, for the time being, the very character of a people who, by nature, are religious. It occurred with suddenness.

This lecture has been given on three continents, and always demand has been made for a comprehensive, reliable statement by someone fully conversant with all the facts, from actual observation, and experience. Realizing the absolute necessity of placing on record an unvarnished report of what was seen, I have attempted to meet the requests made for such a report. There are people at this present juncture in world and church history desiring a similar manifestation that would result in people recapturing the vanished vision of God, and thus returning to the paths of rectitude described in God's Word. Their reader-interest is counted upon.

No literary excellence is claimed for this simple narrative. For many years the writer resisted the inward urge to write a book on this subject, always excusing himself on the ground of inadequate training, trusting that another hand, better equipped, would perform this service for the Church. Gradually, but irresistibly, the impression grew that, having witnessed scenes of such unearthly majesty, I was responsible for the preservation and propagation of these verities, not for the sake of gaining transitory applause or establishing a human reputation, but for the enlightenment and spiritual profit of generations who were, at that time, unborn, but who now, in turn, are clamoring aloud for another awakening among the people of God.

Profound regret is hereby expressed that the name of the Rev. D. S. Jones, who did so much to maintain the spirit of revival in our beloved land, during the years when the revivalist's enforced inactivity deprived the movement of its acknowledged leader, has been inadvertently omitted. No one suffered more, nor served the revival better, than he. We desire to place on record, for the benefit of posterity, as a proof of his unwavering loyalty, that even the large church, to which he had ministered for many years, turned viciously against him. He had ventured, at the dictates of his Master, into "the highways and hedges," seeking "the poor, and the maimed, and the halt, and the blind," bringing them into the Laodicean church where their presence was obnoxious to the self-satisfied.

Heartfelt thanks go to the Rev. John Poorter for kindly scrutinizing the original manuscript and for making helpful observations. Also to Mrs. Hardwick for her "labor of love" in assisting with the final typing of copy.

As this book goes forth to perform its ministry, the words of the bride, spoken to the bridegroom in the Song of Solomon, instinctively suggest themselves as appropriate and fitting: "Come, my beloved, let us go forth into the field; let us lodge in the villages."

CONTENTS

1

REMINISCENCES OF THE GREAT WELSH REVIVAL

D IVINE MOVEMENTS have their birthplace in the heart of Deity. But whenever God predisposes the inauguration of a period of blessing intended for the uplift of humanity, His Church in particular, multitudes of His chosen ones throughout the earth, become mysteriously burdened with the birth-pangs of a new era. Intercessions are stained with the crimson of a splendid agony. Undoubtedly at such a time, God's people pass through their Gethsemane. Throughout the world there are now many thousands of devout Christians yearning passionately for a great spiritual awakening, convinced that only a mighty effusion of the Holy Spirit among the tormented nations can produce the turning point in the history of this distracted planet.

These reminiscences are sent forth in the prayerful anticipation that earnest Christians may experience a strengthening of the faith, knowing that, although the "vision may tarry," it will surely come. Every unbiased person must turn away in despair from endless discussions and abortive conferences, arranged often with a full fanfare of trumpets, concluding in "smoke" and confusion. They only demonstrate that the ailments afflicting humanity from age to age are entirely beyond the capacity of human ingenuity to heal. World cataclysms frequently have resulted in great awakenings of a moral and spiritual character. History proves that national calamities, such as wars, epidemics, droughts, famines, and pestilences are themselves but precursors of better times. Heart-breaking distresses, permitted by God, have been known to lead multitudes into the valley of humiliation. Humanity is sorely afflicted with an enormity of piled-up sorrows. Wistful longings are created in the hearts of the most concerned Christians for a speedy repetition of past history. What of present-day omens?

During past European wars, when fears of invasion created sleepless anxiety in the hearts of the inhabitants of Britain, evangelists of the Whitefield-Wesley type traversed the country with their flaming evangel, asking "repentance toward God and faith toward our Lord Jesus Christ." So great was the moral impact upon the character of the people that the course of British history was changed. George Frederick Handel composed his deathless oratorios at the time when the football of Napoleon on the continent of Europe made the nations tremble. Following immediately upon the tragic days of the South African War, Wales experienced one of the greatest revivals in the history of the Church since apostolic days. David Lloyd George, Earl of Dwyfor, then Prime Minister of Britain, frankly confessed, after World War I, that "nothing less than a great spiritual awakening among the nations could possibly enable the leaders to iron out the appalling difficulties harrassing their minds day and night." Nourished and reared in the atmosphere and tradition of revival, he knew what he was talking about.

The Welsh in past generations experienced spiritual quickenings almost in every decade. Wales earned the envious title, "The Land of Revivals," in addition to "The Land of Song." As in the Book of Judges, so in the history of this little nation, God raised up men of inflexible conviction and great audacity. They went into "the highways and byways" with the divine message consuming their very souls. They called upon the people to repent "in dust and ashes." Names such as Vavassor Powell of Radnor, Griffiths Jones of Llanddowror, William Williams of Pantycelyn, Howell Harris of Trevacca, Rowlands of Llangeitho, Christmas Evans of Anglesea, John Elias of Lalngefni, are forever enshrined in the heart of the Celt. Richard Owen of North Wales, whose spiritual torch was kindled in the Moody-Sankey meetings, roused his compatriots to a deeper consecration. He himself burned out completely at the early age of forty-one. He preached to crowds that would give him no peace.

Perhaps the name of Evan Roberts is the most fascinating of all our honored revivalists because of both worldwide publicity and strange happenings reported to have occurred in his meetings. From the ends of the earth, men and women in all ranks of life, representing different religions, came to Wales to witness personally the strange phenomena. Some criticized, and carnally minded sceptics scoffed. People thronged the churches day and night, far beyond the registered capacity of such buildings, without any decrease for months on end. Mr. W. T. Stead, the intrepid editor of *Review of Reviews,* followed the revivalist for a whole week, attending every service. Writing to one of London's periodicals, he declared in all seriousness that he "could find no trace of the devil in Wales at the present time."

In all Wales, songs of praise raised in ceaseless chorus from the burning hearts of countless thousands were heard in homes and churches and even in the coal mines. There are few, if any, parallels with this mighty outpouring of religious fervor, bringing a whole nation to its knees at the foot of the cross in adoration and praise. It was a fearfully glorious sight, an awe-inspiring spectacle which can never be erased from the memory. Thousands found in all circumstances of life testified in later years that at this crucial time they were "transplanted from the kingdom of darkness into the kingdom of his dear Son."

Let us think of the instrument used by God during this period of blessing in order that we may be wisely instructed in the mysterious, yet majestic, ways of the Divine Spirit, when another such visitation is granted to the Church of God.

2

THE REVIVALIST

G OD hath chosen the weak things of the world to con-
found the things which are mighty," is the classic
expression of the apostle Paul, writing to the brilliant but
egotistical assembly of Christians in Corinth. They were
busy allocating to themselves leaders under whose banners
they proudly and loudly enlisted, to their own spiritual
detriment. This timely rebuke has provided an example
of the unfailing wisdom of the divine methods in the choice
of leaders and servants for the work of the Church. Human folly projects unwearyingly about the brilliance of
human intelligence. Divine methods, choosing "the base
things of the world, and things which are despised," to
perform the greatest exploits in the kingdom of God,
throw into confusion the calculations of mere man. Thus
they secure undisputed glory forever to the glorified Head
of the Church, our Lord Jesus Christ.

Mr. Evan Roberts came of humble origin. His parents
were of the ordinary good, solid, religious type, steeped
in Calvinistic theology; proud of the purity of their home
life; glorying in their church life; scrupulously jealous of
their moral life. One owes an incalculable debt to the
atmosphere pervading such a home. "Island House," stood
on the banks on the river "Llwchwr," where he and his
friends used to bathe and boat continually. Visitors from
all parts of the earth came to view the unpretentious cot-

tage, during the years following the revival in Wales. It was the constant rendezvous of the curious. All his acquaintances admitted the unquestioned sincerity of Mr. Roberts from his earliest days. Diligent in his attendance at "the means of grace," he was unusually serious and solemn in his outlook on life's problems, persistently studious in his reading of the Scriptures—indeed, the Bible, we are told, was his unfailing companion wherever he went. Following the calling of a coal miner, he was once in a minor colliery explosion when a page of his priceless Bible was scorched by the fiery elements. Stranger still to record, it was the words in II Chronicles 6 which lay open at the time of the disaster, where Solomon prayed for revival, and which experienced the scorching tongue of devouring flame. When Mr. Roberts became world-known, a picture of this Bible went around the world.

Was this young man always dreaming of revival? The incident cited seemed prophetic. Once, we are told, he heard a sermon on the words, "But Thomas was not with them when Jesus came." It is reported that those words made an ineffaceable impression on the mind of the youth. Perhaps we find in this incident the secret for his unflagging zeal for the services of the sanctuary. Never did he turn back. Loughor, the birthplace of Mr. Roberts, is a small hamlet situated at the westerly end of the country of Glamorgan, separated from Caermarthenshire by the wide, graceful sweeps of the river Llwchwr (the Celtic word for Loughor). It boasts the existence of several Nonconformist chapels—is there a single Welsh village that does not?—a good day school, and a village hall, a recent acquisition where modern youth assemble for the free discussion of current events. It is a local parliament. There are in the vicinity coal mines where Evan Roberts worked as a lad. Beyond the estuary gleams the golden coast of the glorious Gower Peninsula, famed for beauty.

When the revival burst forth in all its glory within the walls of Moriah Calvinistic Methodist Chapel, the unsophisticated inhabitants of the smug hamlet were like them that dreamed—they seemed to have been aroused out of the sleep of ages. Staggered by the strange, unheard-of sights, they wondered what was happening. Before they had completely recovered from surprise, the name of the village, Loughor, had become famous overnight.

For some years, the mind of Mr. Roberts had been turning in the direction of the Christian ministry. His spare time was avidly devoted to reading such literature as would assist in the preparation of his lifework. Although his friends "with one consent" acknowledged his undoubted religious sincerity and unspotted moral character, there does not appear to have been manifested, to the observant eyes of vigilant church leaders, any outstanding oratorical gift or special expository brilliance, such as is universally expected in Wales in a candidate for such an exalted office. Evan Roberts quietly persisted in the pursuit of his dream. Everything religious secured preëmnence in his mind and heart. Every one of his acquaintances concluded "that Evan intended to be a preacher."

Contrary to the usual nature of a young lad, he does not appear to have enjoyed overmuch the impish pranks of the casual village boy. That was a great pity. For if a lad is capable of much frolic and fun and harmless naughtiness, there are often possibilities lying dormant in his nature for accomplishing great good. In saying that we are thinking of the intrepid tinker of Bedford, whose proverbial genius, used in wickedness in his unconverted days, resulted, when consecrated to highest service, in perennial blessing to God's children everywhere. Our revivalist seems to have been noted for his undemonstrative, studious habits when other boys romped and roamed, his reserved nature, and perhaps his religious inclinations, held him in a vise-like grip. Nature seems to have taken a queer turn in him. But who can judge in these matters? "There is a way the eye of the vulture hath not seen," declares the Book of Job. This may be one of them. That being so, even the keenest intellect lies prostrate before the majestic mysteries of Divine Providence.

One thing is certain—this particular young man was different from contemporaries. Was God already preparing him for the thrilling events lying immediately ahead, beyond his ken, when his name would be honored and talked of to the ends of the earth? In this case, assuredly, the end justified the means. Evan proceeded with his studies in an unpretentious manner, undisturbed by the opinion of others, favorable or unfavorable, and, in due time, the church at Moriah recommended him for the work of the ministry. This necessitated a preliminary period of study at the Newcastle Grammar School, where something took place which completely changed the current of his life, making him famous among the brilliant revivalists of Wales.

Evan Roberts carved for himself a niche in the Hall of the Immortals. "Behold, how great a matter a little fire kindleth." It would necessitate the eloquence of the golden-mouthed Savonarola, or the facile pen of the dramatist-poet of Stratford-on-Avon, to describe adequately the glorious triumphs which followed the unceremonious departure of this young man from home. His avowed object was to pursue his ministerial studies, which, as we shall endeavor to portray later, never materialized. "O the depth of the riches of the wisdom and knowledge of God! How unsearchable are his judgments, and his ways past finding out. . . . Who layeth the beams of his chambers in the waters: who maketh the clouds his chariots: who walketh upon the wings of the wind." Reverently we bow before the majesty of God's awful throne. Insignificant occurrences are sometimes advance intimations of earth-shaking events. Sometimes we find that infinitude lies buried within the bosom of a trifle. When a "still small voice" whispered to Augustine, "Take, and read"— such a trifling occurrence—did anyone dream that the Church of God was about to be honored with one of the most brilliant preachers of all time? Did Wesley have a premonition, as he sauntered into that unadorned Moravian church in London's Aldersgate Street to hear pious Peter Böhler read Luther's commentary on Romans, that something would happen, ultimately sending a thrill of new life throughout Britain, and later, throughout the New World? Millions have since blessed God for that incident. Spurgeon found the snow so heavy upon the ground one Sunday morning that he decided to attend service in a little Methodist Church—an unorthodox thing for him to do, as he later confessed. But the unlettered local preacher had a good text that morning—"Look unto me, and be ye saved, all the ends of the earth." Whatever may be thought of the sermon, that humble unknown man was unconsciously used of God to bring into the ecclesia another Paul. Many avow that when that Spurgeon lad in his teens was brought to Christ, the greatest preacher since apostolic days was converted. Evan Roberts crossed his Kedron to his Golgotha in a similar way. Here is the simple record of the happenings leading up to the mighty revival.

Seth Joshua, a name with a Hebrew tang to it, came to Newcastle Emlyn to conduct an evangelistic campaign under the auspices of the Calvinistic Methodist Forward Movement, a movement which had been recently inaugurated by the devout men of that denomination, who had long felt the need of doing something aggressive in order to reach and save the large non-church-going masses thronging Welsh mining towns and villages, Dr. John

Pughe being the chief instigator. Mr. Joshua was their
pioneer evangelist. He too, had been saved from a life of
profligacy through, I believe, the instrumentality of the
Salvation Army. Seth Joshua was every inch a "man of
God." Every heartbeat had been dedicated and consecrated
to the service of the Highest. This tribute is borne to
his fadeless memory by this author, who enjoyed intimate
fellowship with him in his later and riper years of Christian service and owes much to him.

The principal of the grammar school, John Phillips,
using his great influence over the boys, earnestly advised
them to attend the services whenever their studies permitted. Evan Roberts, so Mr. Phillips informed me in later
years, was evidently impressed by the definiteness and
fervor of the preacher. There seemed to be a strange,
strong, new note about the messages by which he was en-
tranced. Night after night found him a most attentive
listener, without demonstrative commendation. Fellow
students, however, felt convinced that within his bosom
"deep was calling unto deep," soon to break forth in a
Niagara of blessing, submerging a whole nation. But the
Newcastle Emlyn campaign concluded without any spontaneous manifestation of blessing. Indeed, Mr. Joshua
told me that he was somewhat disappointed with the results—everything seemed hard and the people entirely
unresponsive. He was permitted to live long enough to
enjoy to the full the blessings and glory of it.

From that town, the evangelist moved to another smaller
neighborhood on the coast of Cardigan Bay. Here "the
fire of the Lord fell and consumed the burnt-sacrifice, and
the wood, and the stones," leaving behind it a few handfuls
of sacred ashes as a memorial. Several of the grammar
school students arranged to be taken to the place where
the services were held. Among them was Evan Roberts,
unconsciously approaching his holy Moriah. Reports

differ somewhat regarding the occurrences at this memorable service. It appears that Mr. Joshua had experienced special hardness and difficulty in preaching. He was extremely sensitive and temperamental by nature. Those who knew him intimately would say that he was peculiarly influenced by the atmosphere of a service.

Almost in desperation, the evangelist prayed fervently at what seemed to be the close of the difficult meeting, "Bend us—bend us—bend us, O Lord!" Speaking humanly, many believe that this very sentence gave birth to the revival. It became famous. Evan Roberts repeated it times without number. A young woman sprang to her feet in terrible soul-agony—Maggie Evans, if my memory serves me right. At this moment, the silent form of a young man rolled off his seat into the aisle. He appeared to be only semi-conscious. God alone knows how the miracle happened. A lady sitting opposite the young man assured me that he lay prostrate for a considerable time on the floor of the church, sweating profusely. Nothing seemed more certain but that he would die on the spot. Well, he did die spiritually. But he "rose again in newness of life" in Christ, to lead thousands through a similar experience. Suddenly new life had been infused into the campaign. All through that night and the following day, indeed for several successive days, the services continued without any signs of weariness. Evan Roberts was to all appearances a new man after this experience.

Returning to school after this phenomenal baptism, studies for the future revivalist were more than difficult —they seemed utterly impossible. He discovered to his amazement that something had happened and now concentrated book-work was a mere drudgery. Day and night, without ceasing, he prayed, wept, and sighed for a great spiritual awakening for his beloved Wales. Hours were spent in unbroken, untiring intercession, to the chagrin of those who did not understand the symptoms and secret of soul-travail. One thing became clear to him—study was impossible for some unaccountable reason. He had to surrender unconditionally to this overwhelming, mysterious impulse, surging through his sensitive, awakened soul. A vision was given him at this time, so we were informed, in response to these passionate, persistent petitions. It was that a great revival was about to break forth that would be felt to the ends of the earth. This encouraged him tremendously. Although a young man of fine physique, his strong body felt the strain of this crushing burden. Heavenly power swept over him as he pleaded for a lost world, lost beyond hope, and no one to weep for it. Could he continue his studies with this load burdening him night and day, granting him no respite? No! He must go and tell his friends. Others must hear about it even if he died in the effort of proclaiming the glad tidings. Whatever the cost, go he must. It was a tragic moment for him and multitudes of others. Few know the agony of such great decisions. Wycliffe, before his traducers—Luther defending the gospel in Worms, William Carey deciding for India, Hudson Taylor venturing out by faith to save the submerged millions of tormented China—moments such as these never die. Evan Roberts was compelled to turn away from what appeared to be his lifework—preparation for the ministry—to lead a nation to Calvary.

"Go home," said the Holy Spirit to Evan Roberts, "and tell the young people of your church what great thing has happened to you." Immediately, without consulting or pandering to flesh and blood, he went. When our Lord visited His home town of Nazareth, "He could do there no mighty work . . . And he marveled because of their unbelief."

3

THE REVIVAL

THIS REVIVALIST was tested in that way, but with different results. Such is God's amazing grace. It must have been a trying ordeal to have to inform his principal of this decision. But Mr. Phillips was a man of keen understanding and sympathetic nature. Perhaps he felt convinced that the "whim" would soon pass—just a transient emotion—after the first flush of the magnetic experience had expended itself. Arriving home for the weekend, Evan Roberts had leisure and opportunity to examine the ground and, in the orthodox manner, consult the elders about the possibility of arranging a service. It appears that he was led to call a service exclusively for young people, so that he might be free to tell them something about the happenings of the last few days and what he had passed through. Accordingly his wish was made known and an announcement made to this effect. Many of the youth of his acquaintance, convinced that Evan had something unusual that he wished to disclose, came in large numbers, full of animated curiosity. Had such a thing been known before? Not to their knowledge. What momentous hours those were that preceded that service! Can we imagine the tense anxiety of the youthful leader? But no one ever surmised or anticipated what the far-reaching results would be.

There is very little evidence to guide us, except for disjointed reports given by the young people who were present. They reviewed the occurrence in the light of a movement that shook the nation from center to circumference. Very simply, and without any attempt at producing effect, Mr. Roberts rehearsed solemnly and deliberately his experiences, emphasizing the deep hunger of his own heart for a new Britain for God and for a deeper knowledge of the work of the Holy Spirit within. "Not by might, nor by power, but by my Spirit, saith the Lord of Hosts," were the words impressed upon his mind, as he tried to unfold the mysterious dealings of the gracious Spirit with him. Slowly and quietly—for it must be emphasized that fluency of speech had never been a marked characteristic of his—he spoke of the deep things of God and Christ, the hours passing quite unobserved, while tears coursed uninterruptedly over the cheeks of the listeners. People passing by the church commented freely and wonderingly upon the unusual spectacle of the lights burning in full blaze at such an hour. What did it mean? Inside the building strange things were happening. Young men and women who had never been known to speak openly of any experience of saving grace stood and testified fearlessly. Others were bowed in prayer. Some sang the hymns of Zion. Tears, sobs, sighs, and songs of praise were intermingled, continuing until near midnight. The happy throng dispersed in all directions, somber midnight gloriously disturbed by the psalms of the sanctuary. Next day the village was agog.

When Mr. Roberts arrived for the pre-arranged service next evening, the chapel was besieged with curious worshipers, hardly knowing what would transpire. This chapel was not closed afterward night or day for many months, we are told. When it became known that some of the outstanding characters of the neighborhood had been converted after withstanding gospel appeals of eminent preachers for a lifetime, and that these were declaring new-found joy and faith without shame or fear, the excitement became tense. Rumors sped far and wide. Down in the bowels of the earth, miners not only discussed the services but actually sang boisterously the grand old hymns taught them in their childhood, and almost forgotten through sin.

Everything sprang into new life. Former blasphemers were the most eloquent, both in prayer and praise. These men appeared to be making up for lost time—"the years that the locust hath eaten" (Joel 2:25). Drunkards forgot the way to the saloons, which in fact were empty in a few nights. All the former inebriates were busy worshiping. Scores of the most respectable young people of the churches, who had previously never entertained such a thought, joined together and preached in the common, where gypsies usually camped. There they showed the benighted ones the simple way of salvation. Nothing daunted or discouraged them. Was it not the "new wine" of the kingdom that made them bold and merry of heart? It was the young people who responded with greatest alacrity to the searching challenge of absolute surrender and consecration to the service of the Lord. Wherever they went, the very air became vibrant with songs of praise. Hundreds of them, thrilled with an experience to which they had hitherto been strangers, scattered the "divine flame" recklessly abroad—to be seen once in a lifetime! But it was a wonderful privilege to have witnessed, at least once, a land in the throes of revival. God has thus vindicated Himself, leaving His Church without an excuse. He is the same—"I am the Lord, I change not."

Personally known to me was a man who had acquired such proficiency in swearing that even his old companions turned away from him as he blasphemed with frightful vehemence. As a youngster, he had attended Sunday school regularly and thus had accumulated a rich store of Scripture knowledge, which made him the envy of many. To every appearance, he was a most promising Bible student. Alas! as he developed into manhood, he became a ruthless blasphemer. His very knowledge of the Scriptures enabled him to swear with vitriolic fury. His co-workers in the mine moved to a distance when once he commenced to swear. This foul-mouthed man was one of the first to break the silence by bursting into agonizing prayer. Let it be added at once, he was as eloquent in prayer as he had once been in profanity. It was thrilling to hear him addressing Jehovah at the throne of grace. His conversion astounded the neighborhood, as Saul's change staggered the early Church. Everyone marveled at the skill with which he strung long Scripture passages together at the mercy seat—another tribute to the efficiency of Sunday school tuition!

At every service the evangelist emphasized the sentence, "Obey the Holy Spirit." It was his special word to the Church of God. Congregations were urged to sing, pray, or testify, just as they were moved. Human prudence suggested that the meetings would assuredly end in riotous confusion. But human reasoning went far astray in its predictions. They did nothing of the kind. No human agency controlled the services; it had been customary for one person to control the worship of the sanctuary. Here was something entirely new. "Where the Spirit of the Lord is, there is liberty." This was bewilderingly strange to those who had been nurtured under orthodox methods. Nothing like it had ever happened before—at least, not in Wales. Past revivals, even the 1859 revival to which many made hallowed reference, was a very different movement from this one. David Morgan, of Ysbutty, its great leader, had swayed the people by his preaching. Thousands were brought to Christ through his instrumentality. It was not so with this movement. "Obey the Holy Spirit . . . Be filled with the Holy Spirit . . . Do not grieve the Holy Spirit by disobedience"— Evan Roberts reiterated those words tirelessly. Men, women, and even children, came under the spell of the message. Incredible things happened as a result. In the homes, on the highways, down in the coal mines, in business houses, and even in the schools, hymns were sung.

By the end of the week, reports were reaching newspaper offices describing the unusual scenes witnessed in Moriah Chapel. When fragmentary references commenced to appear in the *Daily Press,* people at a distance began to rub their eyes with wonder, for it was not customary for the newspapers to give special prominence to religious meetings. Wonder gave way to astonishment. Astonishment soon developed into inquisitiveness, and this resulted in a somewhat morbid curiosity, constraining the masses to come and see for themselves whether these things were correctly reported. Can you imagine the crush that followed? No building could possibly accommodate the throngs that were keenly anxious to verify, or contradict, the rumors that were circulating.

The second Lord's Day found all the churches in the immediate neighborhood crowded. Young men and women were so completely roused, so quickened in their spiritual experience that they could not possibly remain passive in their seats. Thrilled with an exuberance never experienced nor even dreamed of, they felt compelled to give expression to the joy that was carrying them forward triumphantly, regardless of custom or tradition. Orthodox services were out of the question. Choruses were sung. Incomparable old Welsh hymns, taught them in their tenderest years and expressing the evangelical faith of the saints of bygone days, were repeated over and over again. The words possessed a new meaning in the light of new experience. Prayers, animated by a burning passion, such as were offered, had not been heard by that generation—living, powerful, fervent intercession that brooked no refusal, if human judgment is permissible in a personal, sacred matter.

This thrilling sight was soon to be seen in hundreds of other places. It was well for those young enthusiasts that there were leaders blessed with sufficient spiritual intuition to discern that this was a movement divinely ordained and destined to influence for eternity young lives within the churches. Had the ministers and deacons of the various congregations taken a recalcitrant view, one trembles to think what would have happened. It was a precarious situation. They must have been convinced that this visitation was the direct, though long delayed, answer to the faithful prayers of godly parents, long burdened because of the spiritual drought everywhere apparent. They might not quite understand, but they were at least gracious and spiritual enough to refrain from cruel, biting criticism. Knowing their Bibles, they also realized how extremely dangerous it was to place uncircumcised hands upon the Ark of the Covenant. Were not the Bethshemites smitten? (I Sam. 6). Ananias and Sapphira tampered with holy things to their eternal dishonor (Acts 5). Sights witnessed hourly were like to Pentecostal scenes. Some mocking said, "These men are full of new wine" (Acts 2:12, 13). Therein lies the danger of superficial judgment indulged in by carnal, unsanctified minds.

Whatever men thought, incidents constantly witnessed in this revival could not have been humanly manufactured. "Big" men unblushingly cried aloud in public for salvation. "Lord, save, or I perish!" exclaimed a distracted soul. "God be merciful to me a sinner!" called out another. "What must I do to be saved?" another passionately asked. The fine voice of a young man recently awakened sang,

"I will praise Thee for ever and ever, for saving a rebel like me." A young woman, with tear-stained face, thrilled the people with "Oh, the Lamb, the bleeding Lamb, the Lamb of Calvary; the Lamb that was slain, now liveth again to intercede for me." The congregation burst forth with, "Here is love, vast as the ocean; loving-kindness as the sea," and "Crown Him Lord of all." There was neither tediousness nor weariness experienced by the people.

Newspapers at last became aware of the possibilities of splendid "copy" for their dailies. Reporters arrived and gradually this news assumed such importance and dimensions that other items, even the Russo-Japanese war, were relegated to less conspicuous columns. One of the supreme miracles of the movement was its capture of the press. All over the world people clamored for news. Still the world wanted more news of Evan Roberts and his doings! Many spiritually minded people lamented this fact, persuaded that many of the sketchy reports detracted from the reality and solemnity of the work. Snatches of prayers that were perfectly natural in their own environment were telegraphed all over the globe, creating unseemly superficiality in the heart of many an inexperienced young convert. Unconsciously they became proud of the fact that their prayers were important enough to be reported and broadcast. It was not good. During these strenuous day and night vigils, Mr. Roberts had little leisure to sleep, eat, drink or even to change his linen, like the men of Nehemiah's days (Neh. 4:23). He had become the center of interest, although others assisted materially in the progress of the work. There was Dan his brother, Mary his sister, and a vast number of young enthusiasts too numerous to mention. With ever increasing momentum the movement advanced, creating unprecedented excitement among the churches and the secular institutions outside.

4

VISITING THE ABERDARE VALLEY

IN THE MIDST of the Loughor turmoil, something suddenly occurred causing Mr. Roberts to stretch his
spiritual wings, and increase his sphere of influence and
service for the Master. A church of his own denomination
in Trecynon, a suburb of the mining town of Aberdare,
had read accounts in *The South Wales News* and *Western
Mail* of the work of grace taking place in Loughor. For
some reason, which can only be described as one of God's
glorious accidents, their appointed minister for that particular weekend had canceled his engagement. Someone
ventured to suggest, perhaps timidly, that the young revivalist be invited to occupy the pulpit. That was the limit
of their intention. Believing that he was led by the Holy
Spirit to do so, Mr. Roberts accepted. No one doubted
later the reality of this divine guidance. Early Sunday
morning, after having spent the whole of Saturday night
conducting—if that is a correct term to use in view of
what followed—the revival, he arrived practically unan-
nounced. He was accompanied by two young lady converts mightily inspired by the revival and brimming over
with the joy of the Lord.

They arrived at Bryn Seion Church quite a while before
the scheduled time for the ordinary morning service. From
the moment they entered the building, these young enthusiasts rehearsed and described some of the marvelous scenes

witnessed in their village. They exhorted all present to "be obedient to the Holy Spirit" when they came together for worship. It is safe to assume that not a single member of the audience had any inkling of what was about to happen in this never-to-be-forgotten service. There had been only a brief announcement in the national dailies on the Saturday morning, giving a colorful description of the Loughor meetings and suggesting that Mr. Roberts might be leaving for Trecynon, Aberdare, very soon. "Just an ordinary weekend appointment" was the mental attitude of the church leaders as they entered the building. Imagine their astonishment when they found two young, inexperienced women facing them, and in the most moving tones beseeching them to surrender to "the leading of the Holy Spirit." They proved to be two young revival fire-brands.

The sober, sedate Calvinistic congregation that gathered in Mount Seion that morning received a shock. They looked askance when they saw their minister's place occupied by a young man, accompanied by such youthful maidens. Instead of announcing the customary hymn for the commencement of the service, one of the young women burst forth in a spiritual song expressing her new experience, tears streaming down her cheeks. The whole congregation gasped! Before the solo concluded, her partner joined her. What did this mean? was the question on every lip. Like the people in the Gospel of Mark, they felt like exclaiming, "We never saw it on this fashion before." That prim congregation breathed heavily and deeply. But the young minister in the pulpit—for such they all considered him, remained absolutely silent. They observed, however, that his body shook perceptibly as tears coursed down his pale cheeks. Then, we were told, a strange stillness fell upon the people, like the quiet presaging an electric storm. It soon broke when one of the proudest members of that assembly fell on her knees in agonizing prayer and unrestrainedly confessed her sins, creating consternation among other proud, self-satisfied, respectable members. Others followed rapidly and with such spontaneity as to cause bewilderment. How the elders gasped! All over the chapel, men and women, young and old, kneeling in the pews and aisles, claimed "the blessing." Mount Seion, for once, became a veritable Valley of Baca. The great church organ remained silent.

Immediately upon the cessation of those burning confessions, extempore hymns were sung. How the people sang! That service, commenced so inauspiciously, continued without a break all day! There was no dinner hour nor Sunday school. All the worshipers apparently were oblivious to every physical discomfort as Mr. Roberts reiterated the cry, "Obey! Obey! Obey the Holy Spirit!" with overpowering effect. When evening came, the other churches had received the news. The neighborhood seemed to have assembled in this one place, striving to enter the one comparatively small building where "the revival" was. The crush was terrible. What language could describe the scenes inside the chapel! To the carnal mind, unsubjected and unsanctified, it must have appeared to be bordering on pandemonium. The scenes are recorded here just as eyewitnesses reported them to me later.

Although they had been in the church all through the day without respite, the evangelists continued through the evening service as unwearied as they were in the morning. Evidently "the law of the Spirit of life in Christ Jesus" was assuredly quickening their "mortal bodies," delivering them from any traces of fatigue. News of the meetings sped on lightning wings. Consternation took hold of the inhabitants of Trecynon and Aberdare. In agitated whispers and subdued dismay, groups meeting in the streets and homes discussed the situation. "What meaneth this?"

was the query on every lip. Time alone would give the answer.

Wednesday night came before I contacted "the revival" for the first time.

It happened this way: A young man possessing a fine voice was preparing for one of the great contests which have been extremely popular among the Welsh people for generations. For some time I had been coaching him and correcting his deficiencies in voice production. I did not dream that I would meet him that evening under very different circumstances. After his departure, a friend of mine, a professor of music, called at my room very unexpectedly. Usually the evenings were his busiest times; business people crowded his studio for music tuition. Strangely enough, some of his pupils failed to turn up on this particular date, and he came to see if I would accompany him to the theater, or enjoy a quiet stroll.

After a little consideration, my thoughts turned to the revival meetings which were occupying so many serious minds in the neighborhood. I quietly suggested that we go to the scene of the mysterious services. Immediately, to my surprise, he acquiesed and we both began to walk, and to discuss the reports appearing in the *Daily Press* concerning Mr. Roberts. Usually when we met, which was often, we talked of the great composers of bygone days, debating their qualifications or disqualifications. Cantatas, operas, oratorios, sonatas came under survey and delightful hours passed. But tonight it was "the revival." This was very unusual for, although we were both members of the same large church, neither of us was by any means spiritual.

However, we walked and talked of the revival, and our conversation was perhaps unwise, because neither of us had ever witnessed a revival. Our opinions were, therefore, worthless. Like many others who lived before us, we freely ventilated our vain thoughts. Then something happened. My friend decided that he would proceed no further. My persuasive powers availed nothing. After lengthy debate, he decided that he would return to his studio. Equally obstinate, I determined that nothing would hold me back. 'Although "the revival" brought blessing to thousands of his compatriots, the Spirit of God, as far as one could impartially discern, left my friend severely alone. There was no evidence that "the powers of the world to come" had affected him in the least. Had I turned back with him, would I be writing these reminiscences?

When I reached the precincts of Ebenezer Congregational Chapel where Evan Roberts was that evening, I discovered that every avenue of approach to every chapel in the neighborhood was filled with eager people; hundreds were clamoring vainly for admittance to one of the places of worship. Here was an unprecedented sight! Into this swirling mass I found myself projected. Patience ultimately caused me to reach the vestibule of the chapel where Mr. Roberts was and where at the far end of the room sat a deacon who knew me well. Seeing my dilemma, he beckoned to me, proffering me his chair. Knowing that this was my only hope of gaining admittance, and especially of securing a seat, I pushed through the throng in the aisles, until I reached his chair. That generous deacon, so I learned afterwards, had been there for fourteen hours without a break!

With my back to the pulpit, I witnessed a sight that made me feel faint. Confronting and surrounding me was a mass of people, with faces aglow with a divine radiance, certainly not of this earth. For one brief moment my faith staggered, and criticism arose in my mind. But it soon vanished. Critical analysis could not survive such a dynamic atmosphere. One section of the congregation was singing, "O! the Lamb, the Bleeding Lamb." In another part of the building scores were engaged simultaneously in prayer, some were wringing their hands as if in mortal agony, while others who had received "the blessing" were joyous in their new-found experience. Welsh and English were extravagantly intermingled in this service. Language clashes are non-existent where the Holy Ghost is pre-eminent. With awe and fear I gazed upon this scene. Some of the things that reached my ears will never be forgotten.

On the gallery confronting me was the young man who that evening had been coached for the great singing competition for which he had been preparing for months. Could I believe my eyes? Were my ears also deceiving me? With extended arms, his beautiful voice ringing clear and reaching the utmost extremity of the enormous building, he was praying and crying aloud, "Mercy! Mercy! Mercy!" Just that one word! How had he managed to get into the building? What power was constraining him to cry aloud?

There was no denying the reality of that yearning, passionate exclamation. Another soul in another part of the church exclaimed in stentorian tones that vibrated, "Lo, the winter is past, the rain is over and gone; the flowers appear on the earth: the time of the singing of birds is come, and the voice of the turtle is heard in our land" (Song of Sol. 2:11, 12). Who could deny it? A young woman with beautiful countenance and an exquisite voice challenged, "What have I to do any more with idols? I have heard Him, and observed Him." She clapped her hands for joy. An elderly deacon announced with rapture, "With joy shall ye draw water out of the wells of salvation." A Presbyterian minister, his countenance pale as death, stood on his feet and recited: "Who is this that cometh from Edom, with dyed garments from Bozrah?

this that is glorious in his apparel, traveling in the greatness of his strength? I that speak in righteousness, mighty to save" (Isa. 63:1). Underneath the gallery a young man, stammering, drew tears from all eyes as he cried, "W-w-w-hat m-must I d-do t-to be s-s-s-aved?" repeating the solemn question until he must have nearly fainted with fatigue. A most pathetic sight! One realizes the limitations of his human vocabulary when attempting to describe these scenes.

5

AN AGNOSTIC OVERPOWERED

WHEN THIS GLORIOUS spiritual tumult was at its height, there came a sudden calm. Hearing a movement behind me in the pulpit, I looked up. Evan Roberts was on his feet. He looked straight down at me. Our eyes met for a few seconds. I solemnly avow that those eyes searched me through and through. They burned like coals of fire. In a split second, my innermost soul seemed to be laid bare. I feared and I shook. The luster on his countenance eloquently proclaimed the abundance of grace overflowing his heart. Best of all, he seemed utterly oblivious of it. Had there been a cover nearby, I most assuredly would have sought it.

Then a wonderful thing happened—at least, so it seemed to me. Measuring the huge pulpit Bible with both thumbs, he opened it exactly at I Corinthians 13. Not another page was turned. Then, in measured tones he read—not preached, please remember—Paul's magnificent love poem, "Though I speak with the tongues of men and of angels, and have not charity [love], I am become as sounding brass, or a tinkling cymbal. And though I have the gift of prophecy, and understand all mysteries, and all knowledge; and though I have all faith, so that I could remove mountains, and have not charity [love], I am nothing — nothing — nothing." Emphasizing that word "nothing" and repeating it with deliberation and awful solemnity made us all cringe. It was a painful experience for the flesh. There was no attempt at rhetoric. It was just a plain, simple, unadorned reading. But will anyone forget it? I think not. That fadeless scene has only deepened with the passage of the years.

Before Mr. Roberts had finished reading, a clear voice in petulant mood, rang out like the booming of a heavy gun. "I want to ask a question." Confusion would have ensued but for the unruffled calm of Mr. Roberts. He did not look in the direction of the speaker. "I want to ask a question," again challenged the querulous voice. The rude interruption produced no visible effect upon the manner or mood of the evangelist. Evan Roberts appeared immovable. His eyes were closed and his lips were moving. Evidently, he was in touch with his Lord, probably committing the situation into the hands of his Master. To my inexperienced mind, the situation was perilous.

Just then, someone started one of the popular melodies that was much in vogue during the revival, "O! 'tis lovely! O! 'tis lovely! All my sins are washed away." Somehow one expected the building to collapse with the pressure of glory within its walls. Again and again the sweet words were repeated. Spiritual ecstasy lifted the people heavenward. Above the sweet melody came another exasperating challenge: "If you do not answer me, I will come to the pulpit to ask my question." The speaker, a local man, was well known to the majority present. For years he had been associated with a small but conceited coterie of men who arrogated to themselves resounding titles. Ordinary folk called them agnostics. They were, in many respects, very fine individuals who, by familiarizing themselves with questionable literature, had been led into unbelief. All of them were once members of the Sunday school. Later experience proved that the young man figuring in this interruption was one of the excellent among men.

Because no one heeded his interruption, he proceeded to carry out his threat. All evening he had been sitting remorsefully in the gallery. He moved toward the stairs, the crowd hindering rapid progress; his intention was to reach the deacon's pew, if not to occupy the pulpit. It was a defiant action. God has His own way of dealing with defiance and arrogance. As the man came slowly down the crowded stairway, the unexpected happened. As in the case of Saul of Tarsus, on the Damascus road, the Holy Spirit overpowered this man—he would have collapsed on the stairs had not the people upheld him—constraining him to cry out for mercy and pardon. What a scene followed! When the people realized the full import of what had happened, the shout went up, "He has been saved! He has been saved!"

Riotous enthusiasm broke loose. People surrendered to what appeared to be a delirium of religious excitement. Restraint was gone. Tears and laughter were intermingled. Songs and sobs filled the air. Scenes from the Book of Acts were re-enacted. Saul's prostration was viewed anew in the light of the things happening. *"Haleliwia! . . . Praise the Lord! . . . Diolch Iddo! . . . A'r Ei ben bo'r goron! . . .* Crown Him Lord of All!" excitedly cried the delighted people. In another part of the church they were singing, "Come to Jesus, come to Jesus, come to Jesus just now." All over the church sinners were asking, "What must I do to be saved?" Willing workers moved as fast as the crowded pews would allow them, ministering solace to distraught souls. Moments like those do not often recur during a brief lifetime. We were all in the grip of a spiritual maelstrom. Uppermost in my mind was Jacob's expression, "The Lord is in this place, and I knew it not."

"Throw out the lifeline, throw out the lifeline," sang someone, and the crowd joined in. English choruses were taboo in our unilingual congregations. Freely, but shyly, I confess that I had never heard a single English chorus sung in our orthodox assemblies. To make such an attempt would have been rated almost a "sin against the Holy Ghost." Such a statement may seem strange, but it is, nevertheless, strictly true. The only exception would be the rendering of choruses from the great oratorios of the masters, in our Eisteddfod, our famous competitive meetings. But the singing of gospel choruses in another language was unthinkable.

The Celt found it easier to express his deepest religious emotions in his native Welsh language than in the less-familiar English idiom. But this revival burned all linguistic barriers. And, to our amazement, there was nothing incongruous in it. With what appreciation did they sing, "Throw out the lifeline to danger-fraught men," and "Let the lower lights be burning." The Moody-Sankey hymns seemed to take on an entirely new meaning. Revival makes a radical change in our prejudices.

While this commotion went on, my eyes often rested on the evangelist's face, which shone with an unearthly luster, as Moses' face must have done when he descended from Sinai. It was all so strange to me. Never in all my experience of religious gatherings, extending at that time to over a quarter of a century, had I seen anything comparable. As the Lord Jesus, on the turbulent waters of Gennesaret, gazed calmly at the lashing seas so the evangelist calmly viewed the scene around him. Somehow one expected to hear a voice saying, "Peace, be still."

"Will someone go outside? To the left of the church you will find a woman in spiritual distress. Will you help her to find the Saviour?" This extraordinary utterance came from the lips of Evan Roberts. Profound silence struck us all. It was found to be just as he had said. There was a "calm" of amazed wonder! What manner of man is this? was the unexpressed thought of those in that church. It made one feel uncomfortable.

My own thoughts were anything but calm. What power was it that enabled this young man to make such confident assertion? How could he describe the soul-agony of a single individual when he was surrounded by a multitude, and that soul not even within the building? Bunyan-like, my thoughts were "tumbled up and down." Before an explanation reached me, another request came: "There is a young man in soul-distress at the far end of the gallery. He is anxious for salvation. Will someone please help him?" Turning inquisitively around, the people in the immediate neighborhood saw such a young man, ploughed deep with conviction of sin. He was helped. The crowd once more burst forth in the glad refrain, "*Diolch Iddo,*" invariably sung when a soul had been known to "receive the blessing" and to have entered into the glorious freedom of Christ. But the question persisted —how could the evangelist have known? Those persons sitting nearby evidently had been ignorant of anyone in urgent need of spiritual comfort and help. Closer acquaintance with the Scriptures in later years taught us that the prophet Ezekiel did similar things on several occasions when consciously led by the Holy Spirit. Did not our Lord declare on one occasion, although pressed by the throng, "Who touched me?"

It seems that the spiritual intuitions of the revivalist had been greatly quickened when he received the baptism of the Spirit that made him a world figure. Did it not also make him peculiar, in the estimation of many? This became more apparent as the meetings progressed. For instance, in Liverpool some months later, he astounded the people surrounding him by announcing that there was a person present trying to hypnotize him. Next day, glaring headlines appeared in the city newspapers. Leaders of all denominations fulminated at such unwarranted interference by an unsympathetic spectator. Critics of the revivalist endeavored to prove by this incident that Evan Roberts was losing his mental equilibrium.

Circumstances, however, soon proved that their vitriolic aspersions were made too hurriedly. Proof was advanced later that a professional mesmerist, engaged in one of the city's entertainment halls, was actually present with the avowed intention of paralyzing Evan Roberts' power. This extraordinary incident created confusion in the minds of many adherents of the revival. Much that Mr. Roberts did, and even more that he did not do, was reported around the world. Special reporters dogged his footsteps. Night and day inquisitive newspapermen watched every movement, sending each uttered statement to the ends of the earth. This made an indelible impression upon his sensitive nature. God alone enabled him to endure the publicity. It would have ruined the simplicity of his faith, for the circumstances through which he was called to pass were extremely nerve-wracking.

6

A GLIMPSE OF GETHSEMANE

L ET US RETURN to the scene of the revival in Trecynon. During the service in Ebenezer, another striking incident occurred. After forty years, the scene still comes vividly to mind. Mr. Roberts had an experience which I believe was never repeated throughout his career. Prayer was the keynote of his tireless life. Nothing was ever done in a spirit of independence. No action taken or engagement entered into without definitely committing the matter to God. His soul appeared to be saturated through and through with the spirit of prayer. It was the atmosphere in which he moved and lived. He enjoyed uninterrupted intercourse with heaven. Whenever one looked into his face, he seemed to be engaged in intercession. It was an object lesson to all. Prayer was the breath of his soul. When this incident was far in the past he told us that he had asked God to give him a taste of the agonies of Gethsemane. Probably in his later Christian experience such a request would have been unthinkable. He and others who were prominent at this time of visitation were minors or novices "in the deep things of God."

However, the fact remains, and I am a living witness of the incident, that the prayer was answered in a terrifying way. Falling on the floor of the pulpit, he moaned like one mortally wounded, while his tears flowed incessantly. His fine physical frame shook under crushing soul-anguish. No one was allowed to touch him. Those seated close to him frustrated any attempt at assistance which many willing hands would have gladly rendered. The majority of us were petrified with fear in the presence of such uncontrollable grief. What did it mean? What good could possibly accrue from such manifestations in overcrowded meetings? Thoughts of this nature agitated our minds. No one doubted the transparent sincerity of the man, however mysterious the happenings. When Evan Roberts stood before the congregation again, his face seemed transfigured. It was patent to all that he had passed through an experience that was extremely costly. No one who witnessed that scene would vote for a repetition. One wonders whether such hallowed occurrences should be chronicled.

An unbiased observer would conclude that the youthful members vastly outnumbered the older folk in this marvelous movement of the Holy Spirit. They flung boundless energy into the work, holding nothing back. Their youthful minds having been saturated with Holy Writ during the years of Scripture training in the Sunday school, they were enabled to express their thoughts intelligently and scripturally in prayer or testimony as they were led or impelled by the Spirit of God. Even the very young, between nine and twelve years of age, prayed with wisdom and a fluency that sounded uncanny. One young lad, nearly blind, often startled congregations by his prolific quotations of Scripture. Visitors from other countries noticed this phase of the work. They did not hesitate to express wonder in the columns of the newspapers. "Your sons and daughters shall prophesy, and your young men shall see visions," the prophet Joel had announced. Why, then, should any doubtful misgivings invade the minds of men and women well acquainted with the Scriptures? Buoyant youth was expressing itself in psalms, hymns, and spiritual songs, as Paul exhorted. This preliminary contact with the revival convinced me that the Holy Spirit was tapping unlimited resources by captivating these young hearts. Within a few weeks, that fact was brought home to the consciousness of the whole nation, with irresistible force. These "flaming" spirits swept through the black haunts of sin and degradation with quenchless zeal. They rescued fallen men and women whom Laodicean churches had apparently either forgotten or ignored.

In one of the populous valleys, these young men and women walked in procession through the streets, singing hymns and visiting public houses to invite their habitués to come to the revival. Many of the places were completely deserted and others had their trade depleted, if not entirely crippled. In one such drinking place there was one solitary customer sitting gloomily alone. He was miserable because his friends had all been caught in the upsurge of revival. Suddenly the evening air was rent with the jubilant voices of happy songsters just outside the door. So infuriated were the man and woman in charge at the audacity of these zealous youths that they picked up some of the empty ale-pots lying on the empty tables and flung them out recklessly among the happy throng. They thus provided eloquent witness to the depradations made on the liquor trade by the spiritual awakening. Disgusted with the conduct of his host and hostess, the solitary figure, reluctant witness to this foolish, unbridled madness, rose from his seat, joined the enthusiastic processionists, then went with them to the church, there to surrender to Christ! What jubilation followed is more easily imagined than described.

Happenings in churches everywhere made one utterly oblivious of the passage of time. No one bothered about the clock. Hours passed like minutes. The ticking of the sanctuary timepiece was drowned in an avalanche of praise. Think of the frigid attitudes of the carnal worshiper, forever consulting the clock as the ordinary service proceeds. If, perchance, the minister exceeds the hour usually specified for such exercises, looks indicate the displeasure of stony hearts. When a "man of God" receives divine unction for the delivery of his Master's message, a watch on one's wrist may be a positive nuisance. Revival spells the death-knell of sanctimonious artificiality. Frigid regularity, however beneficial in other spheres of life, falls first victim to the impact of any spiritual movement.

When I left the heavenly atmosphere of the church for home, I discovered that it was five in the morning! I had been in the house of God for ten hours—they had passed like ten minutes! Pushing through a throng that made progress slow, I discovered on the outside of the church that there were hundreds of people patiently standing—waiting in the chilly November air. They had been there all night, hoping somehow, sometime, for an opportunity to get inside God's house. Outside of the crush caused by the multitude anxious to catch a glimpse of Evan Roberts, one became instinctively conscious of a beautiful silence prevailing all around. A Presence, invisible but very real, pervaded the atmosphere. The air seemed electrified.

Moving down the road, with thoughts alert and emotions quickened, I started whistling, "Throw Out the Lifeline." As I proceeded on my way home, it became evident that the haunting melody had gripped my heart. Was it my subconscious self? It is an indisputable fact that, under ordinary circumstances, nothing in Mr. Sankey's collection of hymns would have retained my attention for any length of time, for in my years of study of harmony my critical mind had engaged many times in enumerating and magnifying the irregularities in these simple, but heart-searching hymns. As students, we arrived at the conclusion that Mr. Sankey knew next to nothing about the rules that governed musical composition. This created a prejudice in my heart against anything that appeared cheap in hymns of the sanctuary.

Psychologically, a miracle had occurred. My spirit had evidently responded unresistingly to the spiritual atmosphere prevailing in the marvelous meeting from which I had just emerged. Yes! I found myself whistling abstractedly "Throw out the lifeline"—but what was that— could I hear aright? Was my imagination playing hide-and-seek with me? Someone else was whistling. Who could it be at this early hour? Just a moment ago the road seemed deserted, with only my throbbing heart beating time to the little tune that had invaded the sanctuary of my soul. Yes, someone was drawing nearer, someone who had been caught by the same refrain.

Out of the gloom there emerged, to my great surprise, the fine form of a police officer, standing over six feet in height. For a moment we faced each other in silence. Then in jocular mood I remarked, "Have you caught the revival fever too?" Saluting smartly, as if in the presence of a superior officer, he answered, "Yes, sir, it's right in here," as he thumped his massive chest. After exchanging greetings and discussing the wonderful services, we moved in our different directions. The whistling persisted as sound of his footsteps died away in the distance. I noticed that the tune had not been changed—it was still "Throw Out the Lifeline." Never once were we privileged to meet again. I thanked God many times for this six-foot example of fine "muscular religion" at the outset of the great revival in Wales. How many times, I wonder, did he whistle that tune during his lonely beat through the nights? It was my first contact with the revival outside of chapel walls. It certainly was a good sample!

7

EFFECTS OF THE REVIVAL
IN ABERDARE

OUR LARGE ABERDARE churches soon came into the spiritual gulf stream. With the concurrence of the leaders of the town churches and their devoted minister, now in the presence of the Lord, the huge buildings separated for worship were thrown open. Into these churches surged endless crowds. Enthusiasm was contagious. How well it was that at that time there were men of God occupying the pulpits of the large churches! They willingly cooperated with every suggestion for promoting the revival, even to leading the way into the thick of the fight.

Vested interests were aroused to opposition when they discovered that their ill-gotten gains were imperiled. Was it not so in the case of the great Diana in Ephesus long ago, when Asia felt the impact of Paul's ministry? James Griffiths, Silyn Evans, George Williams—these were outstanding in their advocacy and support of this movement in the town and in their churches. Silyn Evans was pastor of one of the largest Congregational churches in Wales and was held in high esteem by all denominations. Bouyant and youthful in spirit he always was, but at the time of this revival, he seemed to be endowed with seven times his wonted energy. A similar tribute can honestly be paid to James Griffiths whose church was always full,

if not crowded, in ordinary circumstances. Although the
people did attend their churches on the Lord's Day, the
weeknight services were neglected. It was reported that
of a church which could boast of hundreds of names upon
its register, barely a dozen persons would be at the weeknight meetings.

What a quick transformation! Mr. Griffiths acted with
supreme wisdom under what must have been difficult circumstances. He had under his care scores of young souls,
newly quickened by the Holy Spirit. They were so over-
joyed with this new-found experience of divine grace that
they could not contain themselves. They felt that they
must express their feelings in hymns, prayer, or testimony.
The old formal way of worship seemed utterly impossible.
For three months Mr. Griffiths hardly preached at all,
much as he loved to preach. He knew that many of the
older members of his congregation were impatient of this
seeming irregularity, although they refrained from expressing adverse criticisms lest they turn some "out of
the way." But the revival went on! We saw that church,
with an estimated seating capacity of a thousand people,
crammed to suffocation on weeknights with souls crying
for mercy. The pastor—I was one of the dead members
of that church—acted with supreme wisdom. Careful lest
he should "quench the Spirit" in these young hearts, yet
mindful of his sacred obligations to other members of his
flock, he evidenced spiritual sagacity and guided us with
endless patience. Time and again, we saw young men
and women led into the vestry, helpless under the power of
the Holy Spirit. It was a nerve-wracking experience for
the pastor, but his well-balanced mind never faltered.
Strange and unprecedented as these scenes undoubtedly
were, Mr. Griffiths carried himself with Christian dignity.

Another great champion of the revival was Mother
Shepherd of the Salvation Army, heroine of many re-

vival campaigns, a proven soldier of Jesus Christ. Her
name was fragrant in Aberdare—had been for over a
quarter of a century. Wherever she went, she carried with
her a radiance that was not of earth. This mighty awakening that came to cheer her in her later years found her
alert and waiting. She threw herself into the movement
with characteristic zest. She reveled in it. In previous
days, she had been a member of the Booth household, a
nursemaid in the home, assisting Mrs. Booth in the rear-
ing of the famous family. When the General decided to
invade South Wales, Mother Shepherd was chosen to
lead the assault on Aberdare. What a leader she was!
the whole town—nay, the whole valley—was shaken out
of its lethargy. She must have been one of the "hidden
ones" who had agitated at the throne of God for a manifestation of divine power in saving grace. Her keen spiritual senses would have revealed to her that our beloved
people, submerged in religion, in the vast majority of
cases were devoid of any inner experience of the gracious
work of the Holy Spirit. Our religion was like Gideon's
fleece without the saturating dew. When the heavenly influences came, infusing our churches with new life and
vigor, she literally danced with joy, as David did long ago.
    This is an appropriate place to pay tribute to Mother
Shepherd's memory. After my conversion, of which I
will write more later, a habit clung tenaciously to me. It
would have wrought irreparable damage to my work in
the Master's vineyard had not this consecrated soul courageously taken me to task regarding it. She did it so
effectually that there was no need for a repetition. It was
painful—very painful. With infinite dexterity, she wielded
God's Word, cutting out a tumor that was paralyzing my
Christian witness. In January, 1905 the work was done,
and after forty-three years, I recall that experience with
gratitude to God. Well done, faithful soldier of Jesus

Christ! This is deliberately acknowledged, in spite of the fact that it left a scar which the passage of years has not been able to eradicate.

The revival went on in Aberdare and vicinity until its impact was felt far and wide. Into the lodging houses went the groups to sing and pray, exhorting and encouraging the most abandoned to "come to Jesus." Kneeling among these people they prayed for their salvation with agony. Early on Sunday mornings these places were assailed with a divine urgency that was incredible. Weaklings were turned to giants. Young women, beautifully dressed, knelt with vagabonds of the road who had casually turned in for a night's lodging. They pleaded with them to "turn from the error of their ways" to Christ, "the new and living way." These people listened with stoical indifference. Perhaps they were stupefied by the unusual manifestation of unaffected concern—a new experience. Yet the witness was courageously given in burning words. As these young people knelt on dirty, dusty floors, surrounded by banana skins, orange peelings, cigarette butts, newspaper scraps, hardened toast-rinds and egg shells, praying for these callous wanderers, the unkempt room seemed to be filled with the glory of God.

They visited homes also and cottage meetings became the vogue. If there was a home nearby whose occupants were indifferent to heaven's claims, permission was sought to hold services there. In this way, the influence of the revival was felt in the poorest dwellings. How those neglected homesteads rang with glad songs of praise where blasphemy and cursing had been the order of the day—yea, and night also—for years! Monetary assistance was promptly given to dress neglected children and feed half-starved families. Eternity alone will reveal the effect of those gatherings. We know even now that the unusual proceedings wrought such a change in some homes and

neighborhoods that all one could do was to exclaim, "What
hath God wrought!"

These things were accomplished through spiritual novices—"things that are not, to bring to nought things
that are." Instances are known to me of rent-books in
arrears, and shop-books burdened wth very old debts—
some, indeed, had been crossed out as irredeemable by
the storekeeper — completely cleared by these youthful
workers. They reveled in doing exploits. Reflecting upon
this phase of the work, I am inclined to doubt the wisdom
of such conduct, since unrenewed human nature is usually
tempted to take advantage of extravagant Christian emotion. Although that fact became patent to keen observers,
the young converts were blissfully unconscious of any
meanness on the part of the people. It was love-work to
them, and love never feels any burden when on active
service for the King of kings.

Aberdare theater-going dropped markedly. Theater-
fans, scarcely ever missing a single play, found their interest waning perceptibly. A sensational change was apparent. But why this "right about face"? It was not the
result of thunderous denunciations by some preacher.
Neither was it in consequence of anyone aggressively demanding the giving up of such carnal pursuits. By the
good hand of God upon us, we were mercifully delivered
from the unwelcome ministrations of cranks propagating
pet theories that would have produced confusion. It was
the undemonstrative voice of the Holy Spirit quietly influ-
encing daily conduct, turning thought into new channels,
producing the instantaneous results that no other power
could have accomplished.

This was not the exclusive experience of any one locality. City, town, and village throughout Wales felt the
same. Newspaper reports told the world how talented
actors and actresses failed to draw the crowds. Foolish

jests about the revival, indulged in by comedians, not only fell flat but aroused indignation. There was no denying the fact that the stage had lost its glamour, the theater its attractiveness, the play its entertainment value. The gifted, often world-famous, performers failed to charm people. It must have been a heart-breaking experience to be compelled to face huge auditoriums with only half the seats occupied.

Another strange effect produced by this revival was the power it wielded over the hearts and voices of some of the leading vocalists in Wales. Many of them, still remembered, went from place to place thrilling the multitudes with their inspiring songs, without the least trace of professionalism manifested in their performance. They sang in other days because they *could* sing. But now they sang because they could not help singing. They refrained from using the productions of the great composers of the past and contented themselves with singing the simple gospel songs of the revival days. "Where Are the Nine?" and the "Ninety and Nine" were favorites.

Reference must be made to names of Emlyn Davies and his no less famous brother, Arthur Davies, both of Cefn, North Wales. Before the revival, the former had had a brilliant Academy training in London, at the Royal College. His name was well known throughout Wales. Obedient to the urge of the Holy Spirit, he went all over the country, singing at revival campaigns, and thus placed unreservedly his great gifts at the disposal of Christ, the Head of the Church.

Arthur Davies must have sung hundreds into the kingdom. For some years he accompanied John McNeil all over the British Isles. The experience gained became invaluable to him in the sphere into which God called him in later years. What a magnificent voice he possessed! There were "ingots of gold" in that throat! Yet he laid all at the foot of the cross, deeming it a greater honor to be a humble preacher of the gospel than to obtain fame and wealth before the footlights. After preaching, his face stained with tears, he would often close in holy rhapsody by singing, "Pass It On," or "Jesus, Oh How Sweet the Name." On numerous occasions to my certain knowledge, worshipers in Gilgal, Porthcawl, where Mr. Davies ministered for thirteen years, left the church with tear-dimmed eyes, held spellbound by the sermon and the song of a deeply spiritual servant of Jesus Christ. The revival did a great work in his soul.

And the world of sport? Even here the great awakening had made its influence felt. In one village the entire football team disbanded because its members had been converted. Another village reported that their team had been weakened because some of its number had resigned —the revival had engulfed them. Newspaper men announced that this was a common occurrence all over the country.

In Aberdare, both soccer and rugby shared honors in popular estimation. But the winter of the revival proved difficult and some of the matches had to be canceled. In some cases, fixtures had to be changed. Public interest had been reduced to a minimum, a condition which produced disappointing effects on the organizers, and especially on the gate receipts. One does not gloat over the fact that healthy physical exercise becomes deranged when its domain is invaded. Sports, or at least physical exercises, are as essential to the body as Christian means of grace are to the spirit. Man needs both. But when revival is abroad, men and women may be pardoned if they become unusually engrossed in pursuit of the latter, since the majority of people give it so little consideration in ordinary times. Both sacred and secular history prove that a glorious outpouring of the Spirit of God can so completely change the current of human thought as to make men and women almost unrecognizable to their companions of former days.

Did not Mr. Moody's visit to the British Isles change the course of cricket history in those days? We are all conversant with the story of the glorious "Cambridge Seven," all famous in the world of sports; they surrendered themselves to the will and work of Christ, venturing out into the world's most difficult mission field of those days (China) in order that "by all means they might save some." The undoubted sincerity and reckless abandon of the Studd family will always be remembered with profound gratitude to God. Something of that nature, although not to that extent, was witnessed in Wales, for the same purpose in all generations.

Dance halls in many places were completely deserted. Young women abandoned the fascinating pastime that had bewitched them for years. They deliberately cut up the expensive frocks of which they had once been so proud, thus making sure that they would not succumb to any luring temptations. One such young woman, well known to me, had such a baptism of power that she became outstanding as a witness for the Lord. Whenever and wherever she participated in revival services, she reminded one of Catherine Booth, mother of the Salvation Army. Many similar cases could be mentioned. It could be said of many of them as the Psalmist spoke of Israel: "Though ye have lien among the pots, yet shall ye be as the wings of a dove covered with silver, and her feathers with yellow gold." How well did they know it! They mounted on the silver wings of redemption, and were covered with the "golden feathers" of divine righteousness.

Impromptu open-air services were held by these liberated souls in the market place, the city square, or the street corner, where they testified "with fear and trembling" of what the Lord had done for them. Sometimes they would go into the railway station and, after securing their tickets for a certain destination, crowd the railway compartments, singing, sometimes praying, at other times witnessing to fellow travelers. Such "uncontrolled fanaticism," as the cold critic would describe it, could not always pass unchallenged. Some of these young recruits knew what it was to be cursed to the face and even spat upon, as they diligently, though perhaps unwisely, endeavored to win souls for Christ. They made tactical blunders. What else could be expected? Bitter experience taught them later that consuming zeal should be tempered by discretion.

8

THE MINERS—BEFORE AND AFTER

PERHAPS the greatest wonder was the transforming effect that the revival produced upon the minds and conduct of the coal miners. A coal mine seemed to be the next thing to hell itself. Infuriated colliers, in moments of senseless swagger, have been known to challenge God to send an explosion to wipe them out. Incredible as it may seem, in boyhood I knew a man to stand beside the miner's tram that had left the rails and curse until he was almost too weak to stand, to stretch himself out beside the derailed tub and bite its wheels. Because the thing that he was insanely attacking made no protest, he rose, went back a few steps, rushed upon the wagon and kicked it several times until he fell headlong on the ground. Then, with infernal audacity, he cursed God for the pain. Such manifestations of imbecility often occurred in the mines where daybreak never comes, and sunshine never scatters the gloom. Nevertheless, darkness cannot hide from the eyes of a holy God the sins that are committed below the earth's surface. No portrayal could do justice to the miserable condition of poor mules and horses, flogged, kicked, and cursed. Sometimes they responded most eloquently with hoofs that sent the sparks flying. Foul language clouded the air of the mine. Poor dumb animals! They did not understand, in many cases, any language but that of the blasphemer.

Some animals were very sagacious. They would respond to kind treatment. If patience and wisdom were exercised in training them when they first descended the mine, they were capable of helping the men. When the doors controlling the passage of air through the mines blocked their pathway, in spite of the fact they were pulling two or three wagons, they would push their noses against the door and force it open for traffic. Thus time and labor were saved. Sometimes when a well-trained animal was placed behind a heavy tub of coal, he would lean his breast against the back of the tram and push it forward rapidly and easily, the hauler walking complacently behind or beside the animal. In one mine near where the revival broke out, horses were brought to the surface at the end of every shift. All the horses when they came up from the mine would be held at the pithead until the drivers came up, usually in the next cage. When all the horses, standing in rank, were mounted by their drivers, they would dash down the road, turn into the common, make for a pond and plunge into a pool of water to receive a well-earned daily or nightly bath. Thus refreshed they were ready for another shift. The riders had to know how to ride through the waters, legs upraised, or receive a cold ducking. What a cloud of dust would be raised when the horses raced for first place back at the stables!

The revival had its effect even on these dumb animals. So revolutionary was the change in the hearts of some of these swearing haulers that the horses were bewildered. They heard singing from the beginning to the end of the shift! Hymn-singing was altogether unusual! Instead of the customary lunge with the steel-sprag, there was a friendly pat. Ah! that was different! How could they work to this new language which they did not understand? They were living in a rarified atmosphere. "Glory to God! . . . *Haleliwia!* . . . *Diolch-Iddo!* . . . Praise the Lord!"

were the new expressions. How could they work without someone bullying them? They used to start up when the driver cursed loudly and fiercely. Yes, they could understand that. But who could understand all this praying when wagons went off the rails? "Come, laddie . . . Well done, Boyo . . . Try again, old chap" were heard when there was a difficult task to perform which did not succeed at first attempt.

But the conversation of the miners with each other had undergone a change also which was most apparent when they met at mealtime. It was then that they had opportunity to open their hearts. Occasionally, as they talked of the revival meetings which they had attended, their souls would be filled with praises and the old mine would resound with their splendid voices as they testified to the goodness of the Lord. No talk of the coming prizefight! Football was not so popular. They would recount the names of famous Welsh preachers to whom they had listened in the past—great men, who had preached great sermons which had produced little effect upon their own moral characters. Nevertheless, those sermons were now being rehearsed with gusto and enthusiasm—they were living again in the memories of these newly saved miners.

On one occasion, we were told, the manager happened to "come around" a mine for inspection, as was the daily custom. These fine fellows were congregated around their food-boxes, lamps stuck in the timber, hilariously comparing their new spiritual experiences. The manager knew that these men were speaking with "new tongues." The change in their manner and speech was astonishing. One of them, touching his cap politely, ventured to ask permission to give his testimony. With trembling voice and tear-stained face, he rehearsed dramatically how the Holy Spirit had guided him to a revival meeting where scores of young men and women were speaking of their joy in their new-found salvation. On the spot, he was so stabbed with conviction that he shouted aloud—"yelled" was the word he used—for forgiveness, which he received instantaneously, although he could not give any detailed explanation of how it happened. His bright, glowing face gave undeniable proof that something marvelous had taken place in his life. He turned to his manager and asked, "Mr. Beynon, have you experienced this? Have you, sir, been saved?" The answer was pathetic.

"No, Tom, I certainly cannot say, like you, that I am saved. Although, as you know, I have been a deacon of my church for twenty-five years, no one ever asked me this very important question, until you did so just now." He spoke with a tremor in his voice and under great physical exertion. Then Tom answered his superior officer, "Mr. Beynon, listen to God's Word. 'Behold, now is the accepted time; behold now is the day of salvation.'" There and then the rough miner, with his equally rough friends, knelt around their manager in fervent prayer and pointed him to Christ, the Saviour of men. On that very spot he was saved through the instrumentality of these simple men. That piece of earth became sacred to the official, to be remembered as the place where he surrendered to the claims of Christ. There was great joy among those colliers. The verse that Tom had quoted had been taught him in his Sunday school days. He did not know where to find it or whether he was quoting it correctly. The Holy Spirit saw to that!

9

MY PERSONAL EXPERIENCE OF
THE REVIVAL

THESE MINERS, when they came to the surface, at the end of their shift, used to flock to the churches whether it was night or day. They always found the sacred places open. Hours were spent thus in holy fraternity in the house of God. Hurriedly bathing, partaking of their meals, rushing through the streets toward the place of worship, they created a sensation, for this was entirely new for them. But it was happening all over the country.

One Sunday evening in our church, as November was drawing to a close, an announcement was made that Siloah Congregational Chapel was open daily for such meetings as the miners on the night shift cared to attend. A meeting for the miners at such a chapel was certainly a novelty, but all were warmly invited. I thought it would be a novelty to attend, especially if these illiterate miners—as many of them were reputed to be—would make known their experiences in the revival. At that time the town was only partially influenced by the revival—the floodtide came later. The twenty-third of November proved to be my day of destiny. It was a Wednesday morning, I believe, when I thought of the services in Siloah Chapel again. Little did I dream that there lay buried in that unobstrusive reminder a veritable revolution.

As I recall, I had no urgent business engagements that morning. There was no presentiment of an approaching crisis in my life. It was like any other morning except that I felt listless and aimless. About nine-thirty, I left my room and walked toward the center of the town, puffing nonchalantly at my fragrant cigar. My thoughts were heavy; an inexplicable sadness was in my heart. When I reached the square, involuntarily I turned in the direction of the main street. On this street there lived a dear friend of mine, an accomplished pianist, oboe player and organist. His home was our rendezvous when practicing some of the oratorio solos for our great competitive meetings. Scarcely ever did I pass that door without entering. As I was passing, my friend came out, hailed me joyfully, and urged me to come in for a song. But there was no song in my heart, so I declined, and sauntered aimlessly onward.

Reaching the end of the street I hesitated, not knowing which direction to take. There was not the faintest thought in my mind regarding divine guidance, neither had I asked for any. Where should I go? If I took the left turn, it would lead through the poorer streets back to my home. Surely I did not intend to return home. If I went to the right, the road would lead to Trecynon—the place where I had first contacted the revival and where its fires were still burning. No! that did not seem to be my direction. Should I turn back again and visit my friend in the music store? Yes, that seemed to be the way.

When I was in the act of following that impulse, someone seemed to whisper, No, you must go straight forward. Without more ado, I crossed the road, took the street that lay before me, and went on to my Bethel, the church where the revival services were.

Those who are familiar with the neighborhood know

how poor were the houses surrounding this fine Congregational church. Undoubtedly when the church was erected, the locality was different. To reach this church, where Silyn Evans ministered to a large congregation, it was necessary to pass through this neighborhood contrast. I went quietly and unconcernedly, wondering what power was leading me in this strange direction. I was to make the greatest discovery of my life, the greatest in time and for eternity!

Familiar revival melodies reached my ears. It seemed as if an angelic choir had come from heaven to drown earth's sorrows in a sea of song. It was marvelous! Could the singers be miners? The sweetness of the air, "O! say, will you take up your cross? O! say will you take up your cross?" captured me. Yes, I was actually turning the little refrain over in my mind when I met a young woman, greatly agitated. She was well known to me. But what power had stirred her to the extent that she seemed beside herself? This was so unusual for her that I felt startled. Had someone molested, insulted, or frightened her? That could hardly be on such a bright, snowy morning, with the sun bathing the old earth with majestic glory. With an appealing tremble in her voice she exclaimed, "You must come—you must come at once—you must come at once to the revival!" She pointed excitedly to Siloah Chapel, the source of the glorious music. "It is wonderful—wonderful—in there! Come quick!" Amazement took hold of me. For once in my life the power of speech deserted me—I simply looked on. I must have looked at her incredulously for she persisted in exclaiming, "It is wonderful—wonderful—wonderful!" Like one in a dream, I accompanied her to the chapel—or rather, the vestry door. Again the rapture of the singing thrilled me. Lustily they sang

"The law has now been crowned;
Stern justice stands exalted;
The Father calls us blessed through the blood,
And Zion has been ransomed through the blood."

(Such is a rough translation of the words by these inspired miners.) Such marvelous singing, quite extempore, could only be created by a supernatural power, and that power the divine Holy Spirit. No choir, no conductor, no organ—just spontaneous, unctionized soul-singing!

An irresistible attraction, resembling a tremendous magnetic force, drew us inside the vestry. All the seats were occupied, except a few right in the front. Directed by this woman, I tiptoed up the aisle to a seat. It must have been about ten o'clock and lo! the vestry was a mass of worshipers absorbed in the adoration of God. Almost as soon as we were seated, the woman slipped to her knees, breaking forth in such passionate prayer as I had scarcely ever heard, certainly not outside of the revival meetings. No one would have credited her with such eloquence. Indeed, no one had ever heard her engage in public prayer. Words poured from her lips. She was like Gad of old, of whom it was prophesied that "a troop shall overcome him; but he shall overcome at last." The power of God had overwhelmed her, and she was now overcoming. All shyness, timidity, frailty, and human weakness had vanished.

Petrified with fear, I wondered what was going to happen next. I became conscious of one thing, that I was sitting perilously near the "fire"—nearer than ever before in my life. What could I do? Escape? Even if contemplated, that would have been an ungracious act, if not cowardly. Besides, had I not been somewhat familiar with these unearthly proceedings during my visit to the revival in Trecynon? This was only another edition—a second edition of the services which had so intrigued me in Ebenezer. This woman's prayer continued in fervency and passion. Seriously reflecting upon the situation which was momentarily developing into a spiritual crisis before my eyes, I could only indulge in a quiet, inward, mental observation: What a place is this! Everybody seemed to have been affected by this prayer, for all were engaging in intercession, without let or hindrance. One person, with a yearning for communion with God, had mightily moved this congregation heavenward. It would need more bravado than bravery for any man to have dared to interfere with this inrush of divine power.

Singing, sobbing, praying intermingled and proceeded without intermission. When this glorious commotion seemed to have reached a peak, there came through the air a small melodious voice softly singing, "Come to Jesus; come to Jesus; come to Jesus now." It persisted until the people joined in the sweet refrain, inviting sinners to take the irrevocable step that meant salvation. It must have commenced in one of the back seats. But all hearts were soon completely captivated. People joined heartily in the invitation which echoed and re-echoed through the building. It was producing results. In the middle of this singing, a man was heard sobbing and saying, "Pray, pray, pray, please pray for me! I am lost—lost—lost!" He fell on his knees exclaiming passionately, "O God! I am lost—lost—lost!" "Come to Jesus, come to Jesus, come to Jesus just now. Just now, come to Jesus, come to Jesus just now," sang the inspired congregation.

Many of us were now deeply concerned and occupied with this awakened soul, wondering what was going to happen to him. Someone whispered his name, "W—P—." Another picked it up, and passed on the message. Before long, many in that congregation were saying, "It's W—P—." Soon Silyn Evans left his seat and went straight to the stricken man. His usually cheery countenance was grave. Placing his hand upon the quivering form he whispered words of comfort, and the struggling soul became quiet. Lifting up his hand, Mr. Evans returned thanks to God for recovering this wandering sheep who had long deserted the fold for the enticing plains of Sodom, where he had been ruined.

W—P— was now only a phantom of his old self. He was the prodigal son of an old deacon of that church, a godly deacon whose Christian character was known throughout all the churches in the valley. His heart had been broken by this reckless boy who had wasted his substance with riotous living. He had died with this lad's name on his lips. W—P— came back in a pitiful condition, broken in health, ruined in body, destitute, friendless and forlorn. His clothes were worn garments patched and strung together. His toes protruded through the gaping holes of what had once been shoes, now only pieces of leather strung together with cords and bits of old shoelace. An outcast of the town, drink had done its deadly work in the life of this former Sunday school boy. He had not darkened the door of a church for years. His appearance in the miners' service that morning constituted a challenge—how did he get there? What had induced him to come? Had anyone exercised any influence for good upon him and persuaded him to visit the scene of the revival at least once? Or had news of the wonderful meetings held in all parts of the country created within him an irresistible curiosity? We can only conclude that the human derelict had somehow been prompted by an inner monitor to come, with the glorious result recorded.

The young revivalists soon gathered around him. News had gone around the town like wildfire. By the close of the day almost everybody had heard that poor William had been converted in the revival in Siloah. It made great news. His wretched destitution was remedied immediately. The townspeople collected funds to secure for him a new suit of clothes. Underclothes were provided to cover his pathetically shrunken body. Shoes and stockings for his feet were purchased so that in a few hours he was appearing in the streets "clothed and in his right mind." It was a great triumph.

This evidence of the wonder-working power of the Holy Spirit upon this benighted soul produced marvelous results. Christians gave themselves up to unrestrained rejoicing, almost frenzied delight. *"Diolch, Iddo—Diolch Iddo"* sang the people. An elderly gentleman shouted, "A brand plucked from the burning," over and over again. He evidently was acquainted with the case—perhaps more so than any others present.

My poor mind was tossed about with every extraordinary manifestation of the Holy Spirit's working upon the hearts and minds of these people. Sometimes I felt like shouting; again I felt like doubting. At all times I was puzzled. There was no gainsaying the fact that the prayers of these comparatively illiterate people must have been divinely inspired; one felt convinced that simple, ordinary worshipers of themselves could never have composed such sublime sentences as were expressed. The petitions were divinely indited. Some of them fell upon my spirit like red-hot coals, and I was troubled.

My heart became heavy. Almost unaware of what I was doing, I sighed continually. The burden increased with the progress of this service until I felt myself crushed. From some part of the building came the words: "Seek ye the Lord while he may be found; call ye upon him while he is near." Surely He was "near" enough just then, never so near as at that moment. But the voice continued with emotion, "Let the wicked forsake his way, and the unrighteous man his thoughts: and let him return unto the Lord." W—P— had done that. What about me? No one would ever accuse me of having run the gauntlet as he had, for I felt certain that I was far removed from the prodigality of his life. Yet I could not but feel that this call to "return" was meant for me, although I had not the faintest idea how to "return." Morally there was no need for me to do so; but spiritually—ah! that was where I felt pinched and humiliated. Inwardly I was convinced that I had "come short of the glory of God" in spite of my boasted morality. "And he will have mercy upon him," went on the voice; then, as if in a mighty crescendo: "And to our God, for HE WILL ABUNDANTLY PARDON!" These words produced a great effect upon my disturbed mind; I hesitated—Jacob-like, I halted on my "shrunken thigh."

In every prayer there seemed to be Scripture for me— I was literally "mobbed" with the words of God. Beyond a doubt it was the ministry of the Holy Spirit. "Comfort ye my people, saith the Lord," said another. And was I not in desperate need of some comforting word at that moment?

Heavier and still heavier became the burden. Lower and still lower drooped my proud head. Sometimes I felt like falling in a heap on the floor, bewailing my state. Two were praying, a man and a woman. The first was evidently making his great surrender, for he was quoting Scripture: "Ephraim is joined to idols: let him alone." He went on, "What have I to do any more with idols?" Idols of different kinds were troubling him and he was busy disposing of them. His words struck me in my tenderest spot, although the worshiper was utterly ignorant of the stabs. The woman was pouring out her very soul before God. She also had evidently been wandering from her Lord. Was she returning? Listen to her, as I did, with awe: "I was brought low, and he helped me. Return unto thy rest, O my soul; for the Lord hath dealt bountifully with thee. For thou hast delivered my soul from death, mine eyes from tears, and my feet from falling."

She was jubilant at last. Oh, to enter into such boundless liberty!

How it happened I do not know. Whence it came, God alone knows. It has always remained a mystery as the years have come and gone. Visions were talked of among the young converts. Imagination, in some cases, seemed to be running riot. Some vowed solemnly that they were seeing crosses and stars beckoning them onward. No one cared to condemn, although many were incredulous, as I was. Was it something disturbing my sub-conscious mind, flinging upon the screen of my mind a scene of gospel-days with which I had been familiar since boyhood in Sunday school? The passing of the years has produced no satisfactory answer; "the day will declare." The reality of it has lasted through forty-three years of the most strenuous labors in the Master's vineyard, on three continents. My soul was utterly overwhelmed with the sense of awful sin. Deliverance tarried long, while unbelief mocked. My eyes were fast closed. A panorama passed before the eyes of my mind, whether a vision or a mental impression. In those moments I saw more with my eyes shut than I had ever seen in my previous life.

There appeared a huge multitude, varied in costume but differing little in features, interested in a central Personality whose presence was the sole cause of their assembling. Moving majestically among the people, He appeared to speak words of encouragement. Suddenly, a blind beggar, staff in hand, pushed his way through the crowd, and knelt in the pathway of the Speaker crying, "Jesus, thou son of David, have mercy on me!" Some reached to pull him out of the way, but a hand was extended to protect the defenseless man. Standing with royal bearing, the central figure encouraged the people to bring the poor fellow to Him. Again, dropping his staff and extending his hands, the beggar evidently repeated his cry.

Then something within snapped—my bonds were gone. I jumped to my feet, extended my arms, and took up the poor man's words. Oh! how I cried! Was ever such a cry heard anywhere? Desperately, passionately, fervently, I cried, "Jesus! Jesus! Jesus!" over and over again, unable to continue with petition. With that one word, I held on like a drowning man clutching a straw—it seemed to be my last chance, absolutely the last.

"Jesus! Have mercy! Have mercy! Have mercy on me!" I cried. How many times, I do not know. This I do know, that no argument of a psychological nature can ever disturb the serenity of my faith. A sweet voice spoke within my spirit so clearly, unmistakably, audibly, that the voices of all creation could never succeed in drowning its message: "Be of good cheer, thy sins are forgiven thee."

Heaven came into my heart that very moment. Blind Bartimaeus heard the words, "Be of good comfort, rise; he calleth thee. And he, casting away his garments, rose, and came to Jesus" (Mark 10:47-50). My message was: "Be of good cheer, thy sins are forgiven thee." Unlike Bartimaeus, there were no garments to be shed. But there were sins to be banished, and they were banished. There were burdens to be dropped, never to be picked up on any pretense again. But like Peter, of whom it is recorded, "and his chains fell off from his hands" (Acts 12:7), so my sins went. No chain has since been forged that was strong enough to hinder my service for the Master or to retard the advancement of my spiritual progress. Delirious joy possessed my soul instanteously. Henceforth there was no keeping quiet. Revival had swept shyness away. So possessed was I with the "new wine of the kingdom of God" that I, like many others in the revival, seemed to have lost my mental equilibrium and self-control. This great miracle within me must have taken place in the neighborhood of eleven-fifteen, as near as an estimate of the time can be made. According to that calculation, I had been in the church about an hour and fifteen minutes. It seemed to me like eternity, since the burden on my spirit had been so heavy.

Now everything was changed! Had anyone prophesied in my hearing that such a thing could have happened to me, I would have unhesitatingly christened him Balaam, the hireling prophet. Everyone in the service that morning knew full well what had happened to me. And at the time of this writing, there are at least some living who know about it. For instance, the lady who sat at my side, my sister-in-law, is a living witness, although advanced in years. Throughout that service my voice was heard. How could one be silent when waves of joy were submerging him!

Hundreds in that building felt exactly as I did. Worship according to the old dignified order was banished unceremoniously. On and on and on went that glorious miners' meeting, leaving a golden trail behind. Is it not still going on? While my heart beats, that revival service will neither slumber nor sleep. It is fadeless, endless, eternal! Ah! this is something that even the grave cannot stop. "When time shall be no more" this deathless experience will still have the dew of youth upon it. The two converts of that service, though poles apart morally and socially, were like twins thereafter. It was with joy that I embraced my new-found brother when we parted at the conclusion of that eventful meeting.

Before I left the church, a woman spoke words that staggered me. She was known in the town as a spiritual woman, the wife of one of the ministers and highly respected. During the service, words had passed my lips that had impressed her. Under the impulse of the moment, she said that I ought, or that I would, join Evan Roberts in his great work. She felt impelled to say that my lifework would lie in that direction. I had not dreamed that any words of importance had been spoken by me in the several prayers that I had offered, and I never asked her what they were. The secret remains unrevealed.

"*Ap Tudor*," said she, (using the title by which I was known in the world of music, meaning "son of Tudor"), "I want you to promise me one thing. Will you?" Actually I was in a mood to promise anything within reason. It seemed to me as if I would have given away a kingdom, had I possessed one. So I assured her that I would give the promise immediately if the fulfillment of such a promise were humanly possible. Without hesitation she said, "I want you to give all your rich gifts and talents to the service of the Lord Jesus Christ." In a subdued tone I inquired: "Do you think I have any?" With confidence she averred: "God has enriched you and equipped you for His work. Will you give your talents to Him?"

Confronted so suddenly with such a situation—a situation pregnant with solemn consequences—I demurred. Who could blame? I hesitated. No one had ever issued such a challenge. I pondered, calculated, waited. "Will you not give the answer now?" Her voice trembled, sincerely apprehensive lest I should make the wrong choice. Suddenly the choice was made. I declared, "I will give all to the Lord Jesus Christ." Imagine my apprehension when she declared, "My husband will write Mr. Evan Roberts making the suggestion that you should join him." This was more than I could stand. I pleaded with her not to move too rapidly, at least to wait until I had time to find my bearings.

Nothing came of it. The proposal was frightening. I never mentioned it to a soul. Whether the proposal ever reached the harassed revivalist, I do not know. As the days and weeks passed without indication of the divine direction for my sphere of service, I felt relieved. Although I followed Mr. Roberts from place to place, taking quite a prominent part in all the meetings, we never met personally. And yet, some things that I mentioned in prayer had evidently caught his attention and made an impression, for he drew attention to them, spoke on the words, as was his invariable custom, re-emphasizing them in a remarkable manner. Thus he drove the message home to the hearts of the attentive people who would not willingly miss one word from him who spoke infrequently. When he did speak, there was no escaping the import.

Afterward when the revivalist reached Pontycymmer, a town in one of the famous mining valleys of Wales, news reached us daily through the press of the marvelous things that were happening there. Commencing his work in the Calvinistic Methodist Church, the building had in a few hours become quite inadequate to hold the people clamoring to both see and hear. Every chapel was requisitioned for the purpose of at least attempting to accommodate the crowds. Even then, multitudes could not find admission, and people were standing for hours in the cold, wintry mountain air hoping, perchance, that by someone's leaving the church they could push in to witness the scenes that were taking place inside. Exactly nineteen years later, standing in the very same pulpit, I witnessed similar scenes with churches crammed during an evangelistic campaign I was then conducting. Those dear old deacons were never tired of comparing this campaign with the high days of "the great revival."

A new departure appeared in the plans of Evan Roberts after his visit to Pontycymmer. The minister, T. Mardy Davies, undertook to become the organizing secretary of the work, arranging services throughout the country as the overwhelming demands came in. These abnormal demands necessitated someone's taking matters in hand and planning the visits consecutively, so that each might be gratified by

the result. There was then some semblance of arrange-
ment. Evan Roberts followed the plan worked out for
him, and a triumphal tour followed. No king was ever
more honored than this simple-hearted young servant of
the King of kings. Throngs followed him day and night,
making life almost unendurable, until the approach of
Christmas (the ever blessed "Christmas of the Revival,"
as it came to be remembered), when the program mapped
out permitted him a homecoming. No question but that
his soul would be yearning for this. Was it not the place
"where the fire fell"? Was it not the neighborhood where
the conflagration first caught on? Was it not the locality
from whence he had gone to set afire his beloved Wales?

But the homecoming did not mean rest. People had been
waiting, and some of the lively, impetuous young converts
had even dared to pray for it. Who can blame them?
Whatever spiritual experience had become theirs would be
forever associated with the name of their young friend and
neighbor, Evan. Paul's converts in some of the Galatian
churches were prepared to express their joy at a tremendous
cost. Would one blame the young believers in Loughor if
they essayed to honor the man whom heaven had delighted to honor?

The revival in Loughor must have received a new impetus with the return of Evan Roberts—not that there
was any evidence that the fire had been banked during his
absence. Night and day the meetings had continued with
little, if any, abatement. Years later when I was preaching in the district, I was assured that the chapel, now
famous throughout the world, had not been closed night or
day for months. Where is the power that can extinguish
the fire that has been kindled by the hand of God? Let
the Baal prophets try it! "Fill four barrels with water,"
said Elijah, to the chagrined prophets of Baal. "Do it
again! Do it again!" he mockingly urged. "The water ran

round about the altar; and he filled the trench also with water." Here is enough water to damp any fire! "The the fire of the Lord fell and consumed the burnt sacrifice, and the wood, and the stones, and the dust, and licked up the water that was in the trench." That's the answer that God gives. Have you seen a fire that can burn stones? In Wales we saw stoical—stone-icol, to coin a word—hearts, burned by the divine fire.

Certain it is, although he had very little privacy during this visit, Mr. Roberts must have recuperated somewhat during the experience, for he appeared in public, like a giant refreshed.

10

EVAN ROBERTS VISITS VILLAGES
AND VALLEYS

IN THE YEAR 1905 the movements of the revivalist were controlled by his indefatigable secretary, who had the stupendous task of arranging his engagements so as to leave Mr. Roberts free to concentrate upon his work. However, much as we may differ in opinion regarding this particular, we know that his movements for some months, at least, took the form of a mighty pageant. Forest Fach, Cwmbwrla, Swansea, Morriston—all were visited in turn with multitudes following him everywhere. Some would even have "touched the hem of his garment" as if expecting virtue therefrom for bodily healing or for spiritual blessing. It was a "terrible" eminence to have reached—giddy height enough to overthrow an angel! When a human being reaches a place where there is danger of being worshiped, then it is time to "call a halt." Even our Lord found that the Temple pinnacle did not place Him beyond the wiles of the tempter, Satan. The great German Reformer Luther made a similar discovery.

What drew one to Evan Roberts, perhaps more than any other one thing, was the unfeigned humility manifested in all his actions. How long would he last, surrounded as he was by such praise and attention? Ministers from the British Isles and the continent of Europe followed him. Eminent Bible teachers, well-known pastors from Russia and Germany, and world-known evangelists came to "see the fire." Missionaries from earth's darkest regions — India, China, Africa, Egypt, attended and watched with wistful eyes, hoping to catch the flame before their return to difficult, lonely posts. Christian workers from the slums of the big, dark cities, who had borne the burdens of disappointed hopes with gallant chivalry for years, came to "see." They hoped that they would receive a baptism of power that would send them back to their drab spheres with new bouyancy.

At one of the services we saw a bishop, a man of advanced evangelical views whose name was quite unknown to us at the time, who seemed puzzled at what he saw and heard. One London-Welsh minister suggested that this gentleman should be asked to speak. This was contrary to the principles on which the revival was carried on. Had he been long enough in the country, he would have known that. Evan Roberts refused the suggestion. Anyone could speak, if he felt led to do so. No one could speak by invitation.

One can easily imagine how strenuous was the evangelist's life. In the small market town of Neath, the sweltering crowds were staggered by the news that Mr. Roberts would not attend any more revival services for seven days in succession. What did this mean? Many had come long distances to see and hear him. Were they to be disappointed and denied? All that was undoubtedly true, but the revivalist was adamant—no amount of persuasion could prevail with him to alter his decision. Divine instructions had been that he was to remain shut up in the room graciously placed at his disposal by the host who was entertaining him during the visit to Neath. All seemed to be confusion. Not only was he to accept a divinely appointed imprisonment, but he was absolutely forbidden to have visitors. He was not to speak to a living soul during this captivity of the Spirit. Rigorous silence was imposed upon him in the most absolute way. Visits from relatives, friends, or strangers were forbidden. All instructions were to be given in writing.

It is difficult to account for this strange incident. Yet, if we hazard a guess, we may be pardoned. Ezekiel, the Old Testament prophet, soon after he was called and equipped for his lifework, went to visit "them of the captivity of Tel-abib, that dwelt by the river of Chebar, and I sat where they sat, and remained there astonished among them seven days." A little later we are told, "Then the spirit entered into me, and set me upon my feet, and spake with me, and said unto me, Go, shut thyself within thine house . . . And I will make thy tongue cleave to the roof of thy mouth, that thou shalt be dumb, and shalt not be to them a reprover: for they are a rebellious house" (Ezek. 3:15, 24, 26).

The conjecture is that our friend had been reading that Scripture. He would find in Ezekiel a prophet after his own heart and engaged in similar work. Encouraged to trust implicitly the all-wise guidance of the Holy Spirit in all things, it is possible that this special word came home to his soul with such power as to compel the belief that the Lord was leading him to do the same. Many of God's children have had Scripture impressed upon them in a similar way. There is no mistaking the force and power of such an experience.

Perhaps Mr. Roberts needed that "seven days" for quiet spiritual contemplation, in view of the irresistible rush of things. Remembering that he was comparatively a young believer himself, called upon to stand the strain associated with the guidance of this world-shaking event, what would be more natural than that his Lord should constrain him to "turn aside"? He needed very special enduement for this formidable task. Moreover, what about his physical need? He had very little relaxation while at home during that Christmastime. Was this enforced retirement a wise providential provision wherein he could replenish his nervous strength spent without a single thought of self-preservation? Did not our Lord once say to His disciples, "Come ye apart, and rest awhile"?

Whatever the explanation, it must remain a secret. It set the world agog. Even the singularity of the incident added to the man's fame. Everybody was thinking and talking about that solitary figure receiving no friends, granting no interviews, and permitting no interruption to his serious thoughts. Even the host and hostess were excluded from association with him. Many of the thoughts occupying his mind during this time were written down. Some of them were published later by the newspapers. During this period he expressed a desire to visit the Holy Land. It might even have been a passing desire, mentioned without any idea of giving it publicity. But the newspapers were alert. Here was a glorious opportunity for securing much coveted "copy" that would increase circulation! Offers were made to expedite a visit to Palestine, of course, on conditions. All his expenses would be met if he would consent to write his experiences exclusively for one London paper, a religious magazine.

There is reason to believe that the offer was made in good faith. That particular paper had given great prominence to the revival in its columns and would, no doubt, do everything within its power to facilitate the good work in which Mr. Roberts was engaged. One is definitely inclined to believe that both proprietors and editor fully intended to be of service to the movement in Wales by aiding the overworked evangelist to recuperate in this way. A sea voyage through the Mediterranean was not to be despised. Especially acceptable would be a visit to the scenes of our

Lord's ministry and suffering, when all the world was talking "revival." There were universal expressions of gratitude for the offer. It did not seem possible that such an opportunity could be missed. Unanimous public opinion was that it was just the right thing.

Mr. Roberts rejected the offer. Perhaps he had never intended that the reference upon his writing-pad should be taken seriously. It is more than possible that he felt that this was not the time to leave to less-experienced persons the great work entrusted to him. Surmises, one way or the other, lead nowhere. Since he had, no doubt, committed the whole matter to God, who will dare to challenge the wisdom of his action? His selflessness, was, however, patent to all. Few indeed are the number of the people who would have rejected such an offer. But Evan Roberts was otherwise engaged. Pre-occupied with his "Father's business," no allurements, from any quarter and in whatever guise, could induce him to leave the path of obedience upon which he had embarked in simple faith upon the Bible promise, "My grace is sufficient for thee."

Many years have passed since the incident occurred, but it does not seem that this wish was ever gratified. He never visited the Holy Land, as far as I know. Doubtless the offer to defray all expenses could have been renewed many times by the same publishers, if intimation had been received that the famous revivalist was disposed to go. Throughout the years of retirement from active service that have intervened, no expression of desire to visit the Holy Land has been made public. His has been a sphinx-like silence, whatever his inner thoughts.

Foreign travel does not seem to have occupied his thoughts. If he had been so disposed, other countries would have welcomed him. America, there is not the least doubt, would have opened her doors wide. Wherever I have lectured on this subject in the United States, in churches, mission halls, and over the air, many have expressed willingness to arrange a revival tour for Mr. Roberts, if he could be persuaded to put his signature to such a plan. He was evidently convinced that the Holy Spirit had circumscribed his sphere of service. His burden was for Wales. The message entrusted to him was for his own beloved people. Frankly one is inclined to doubt whether any other people were ready to receive a message of such a character at the time. Even in England, many portions of which had been at least subjected to the divine fire kindled among the mountains of Wales, there were churches which flatly refused to accept revival upon these terms. They deliberately "bolted" the doors against it. No such manifestation would be allowed within the precincts of their sacred walls. Today they are infinitely poorer because of it. What country, community, or congregation dares to refuse the enrichment and enduement of the Holy Spirit, as proffered in the sacred Scriptures, without crippling its spiritual activities and sterilizing their Christian service?

When Evan Roberts emerged once more, to take up his glorious work for the Head of the Church, his Saviour and Lord, his advent was awaited with great anticipation. Neath and environs thronged with people who had traveled great distances with the intention of participating in this adventure for God, guided and encouraged by the knowledge that the work would receive a new impetus when the mysterious seven days had expired. Anticipation had intensified the keenness of the scores of thousands who had been blessed through the revival.

Time had been given for people from all parts to foregather. Curious ones exclaimed, "If we could but see him, we would be happy." Anxious souls would say: "If we heard a message from his lips, we would be recompensed a thousand times for all the sacrifice made." Every available building was conscripted for the purpose of holding revival meetings. And they were needed. The streets of Neath were literally swarming with masses of anxious people—anxious in more ways than one.

The small market town could boast of some of the largest churches in Wales. But what were they "among so many"? From one to the other of the large Nonconformist church Mr. Roberts went, paying a visit in turn to them all. People wept as they saw him, so grateful were they to see him in the forefront of the battle again. These services defy description. Pent-up emotions overpowered the people. One man, evidently well-known, judging by the exclamations of approval when he prayed, thanked God not only that the Saviour could "turn water into wine, but that He had turned beer into furniture in his home." Sitting beside him was his wife, alternately clapping her hands and wiping the tears away. Another man proclaimed to the world "that he had been riding in the devil's motor car [they had just then begun to be popular] for thirty years, and was speeding to hell at twenty miles an hour, when Jesus blocked the road and saved him."

These expressions may appear childish when read, but to hear them given in the power and demonstration of the Holy Spirit is quite another matter. Nothing could be more expressive of their experiences than these simple, picturesque sayings. Newspapermen caught them and sent them spinning around the world in a few hours. In one of the churches was seen a beautiful little woman, carrying a tiny baby in her arms, the two of them almost overrun by the surging crowd. Her red cheeks bespoke perfect physical health. She had a small, round, well-chiseled countenance, eyes jet-black and ablaze with a divine passion. Her utterance of the deep soul-stirrings within her overwhelmed the listening worshipers. The hymn which she sang loses its exquisite Welsh idiom in the translation of the verse.

"In the Garden, lone and weary,
Hearken to the words He said.
Let my friends depart in safety;
And imprison me instead.
Here is love, untold, unrivaled,
Wondrous love beyond compare."

Years have passed yet there comes afresh the thrill of that delightful refrain: "Here is love, untold, unrivaled, wondrous love beyond compare." These words were of ancient date, the product of past revivals experienced in Wales. The transporting, transcendant harmony, was the product of the heart and brain of a local genius that had burned itself out in a few but aggressive years. Majestic strains such as these inspired by the Holy Spirit seemed to descend from heaven as the people sang different parts, which they naturally do in Wales. This woman had set them going, her tuneful notes, reminding one of a skylark, were heard above the sound of many voices.

Leaving Neath, the itinerary of the revivalist took him through the beautiful valley that takes its name from the town, the Vale of Neath. Nature has bestowed her loveliest graces upon this Edenic spot, the rendezvous of thousands of tourists and picnickers. Riotous floral beauty meets the eye everywhere.

When Evan Roberts commenced his tour of this valley, following upon his seven days' retirement, it was winter, and a white blanket of snow lay thick upon it. Wintry winds whistled through gaunt-looking trees, clustering along the hillsides. A local tradition persisted, handed down from one generation to another, concerning the heir to Rheola estate. He was engaged in some of the numerous European wars; after returning, he planted trees in clusters to illustrate the positions of the different armies during the crusades.

On the outskirts of Neath stood the picturesque, ancient little town of Aberdulais. Here the revival burned brightly. Mr. Roberts passed through the place on his way up the valley. Reaching Resolven, an enchanting mining village, he found that the Spirit of God was mightily in evidence. The large Congregational church and the somewhat smaller Baptist church witnessed scenes of mighty revival. From daybreak and throughout the whole day, without break and without the least evidence of fatigue, crowds besieged these buildings, intent upon participating in the spiritual blessings that were transforming the life of the nation.

Evan Roberts was coming. It was the topic of conversation among the people, but no one knew beforehand to which church he would come. Consequently, both churches were crowded. The spiritual atmosphere pervading the worship of the people so thrilled him when he came that his countenance seemed to be luminous. Wherever he felt the perfect liberty of the Spirit in a service, his eyes glistened, his face became almost transformed, and his smile radiant. Burdens lifted, sighing fled. Christ glorified— what else mattered? With boyish joy he entered into the spirit of the services. Changing moods were apparent— now the song was in the minor key, anon it was in the major key. Invitation hymns suddenly turned into rhapsodies of praise. A somber "Dies Irae," issuing its dread ultimatum to sinners, warning impenitent mockers of impending doom, uttered by those inspired voices, would resound through the building, filling every soul with unspeakable awe. Sensitive to these changing moods of the Spirit, Mr. Roberts would reflect them in his face. The meetings in Resolven were unique in this respect. And yet, they closely resembled the meetings in other towns, and could be pronounced of one pattern.

11

EVENTS AT RESOLVEN AND HIRWAIN

I WAS AMONG the throng crowding the gallery, but seated on a step, not a seat, in the large Congregational church, when Mr. Roberts arrived. During the service he seemed to be as free from the "burden of the Lord" as a bird escaped from the fowler. He sang blithely with the worshipers around him—quite an unusual thing for him. He was so often weighed down beneath the burdens of others.

Sometimes during the prolonged service (lasting throughout the day) a season of prayer broke forth that overwhelmed all present. Hundreds must have taken part simultaneously. In the gallery, somewhat near to Mr. Roberts, I was led to participate. Mr. Roberts caught some of the words and at a later period mentioned the prayer in a very special way. He emphasized the extreme importance of seeking divine guidance in all spiritual matters, whether great or small. For, as the tiniest pin or socket had its place prescribed for it in the structure of the Tabernacle in the wilderness, so the insignificant details in our lives were woven into a heavenly pattern. Guidance and obedience were the words crossing his lips with almost monotonous reiteration.

I had been for days seeking guidance on a matter of extreme spiritual significance. I was deeply perplexed. Mr. Roberts urged abandonment to the will of God. This I was prepared to give immediately and at whatever cost.

I desired clear, unmistakable direction from God. Unconscious of the importance of words uttered with the utmost simplicity, the revivalist made an affirmation that the course premeditated was the one mapped out for me and which I would have to pursue. The conflict terminated there and then. My faith immediately became robust enough to declare that the victory had been won. There was nothing for it but obedience "to the heavenly vision."

The question was in regard to my call to service for the Lord. When the revival was at its height, many left their homes on the impulse of the moment, claiming to have received a vision which called them to give up all and follow the Lord. Off they went, some to Ireland, a few to Scotland, several to different parts of England. London was a favorite choice because of the London-Welsh population in the metropolis. This exodus of inexperienced novices continued for some time. In a very short time, however, many returned disillusioned. Others struggled on until their slender resources were exhausted, and they were compelled to retrace their steps in penitence, exposing themselves to unsympathetic criticisms. Spiritual people were desirous that the good work should not suffer irreparable damage because of precipitate action of some of the converts. Deep concern was felt when young people were seen to discard restraint and give up their jobs to engage in work the nature of which they were ignorant.

It should be admitted that the fault was not entirely on the side of these young enthusiasts. People coming from other countries were so impressed by what they witnessed that they foolishly concluded that if they could but induce a few of these "firebrands" to visit their churches and towns, to testify and sing, a similar revival would ensue. To advertise the presence of Welsh revivalists, coming straight from the midst of the awakening, would assure large congregations, followed by great blessing—so they reasoned. To some extent, they were right, for the very mention of anyone coming from the Welsh revival to conduct meetings commanded wide attention. People came in large numbers to see and to hear. What did they hear? Once the young convert's testimony had been given, often, with wonderful effect, their lack of religious knowledge and training soon manifested itself, to the detriment of the work. Lionizing young converts, at any time, may easily prove to be disastrous. They are placed in positions for which they possess little or no qualification. So it was that visitors to Wales, impressed by a bright experience and a pleasing personality, and profoundly anxious to see a spiritual movement break forth in their home area, would invite these untried young folk to visit their home churches.

Knowing these things, one naturally felt a restraint when contemplating a similar step. Such was the case with me when entering the chapel in Resolven. After I surrendered myself entirely to the Lord at the challenge in the service in Aberdare, I felt that I would ultimately be called upon to work in the Master's vineyard. This I dreaded, for I positively had no ambitions in that direction. Other projects had occupied my thoughts for years, and all my studies and training were undertaken with a view to the pursuit and fulfillment of those plans. Now it looked as if they were to be crushed, and it was a crucial moment. Moreover, I feared I would repeat the mistake of others who had been blessed in the revival. They had gone forth in many cases and were compelled to return. Was the urge within divine or human? Did it originate with me, or did it come from God? Fully conscious of the consequences of such a decision, I did as the Psalmist did, "I waited for the Lord." "God is our refuge and strength, a very present help in time of trouble." So "I waited" for

Him. Through Evan Roberts He sent the answer. The struggle was ended. From that moment I knew that I would have to take the revival message somewhere other than to my own little country. The time of departure and the length of my mission were still unrevealed, but the greatest conflict was over. My heart was at rest. Resolven will be forever associated with my work for the Lord, wherever I go.

From Resolven, the revival party moved up the valley to Glyn Neath. Here again the "fire" was brightly burning. Crowds walked about from early morning, in spite of cold weather and snow. Nothing could dampen the ardor of these people who were bent on securing divine blessing. Although the pretty village could not boast a large population, it seemed as if the nations of the world were represented, judging by the color of the costumes. Following Mr. Roberts day by day for some time gave opportunity to compare the characteristics of the congregations in different localities. Trainloads seemed to come from anywhere and everywhere. Hobnobbing, rubbing shoulders with and, better still, sitting beside Indians, Chinese, Japanese, Germans, French, and Russians in a spirit of worship was certainly a unique experience in a small Welsh village like Glyn Neath. Why had they come from such distances? To reach these somewhat obscure hamlets was not easy, for they were off the main line of travel. Changing lines, changing trains, and consulting timetables seemed to entail no hardship. Lingual difficulties were completely absorbed in the pursuit of spiritual blessing. People prayed in several languages simultaneously. It was the nearest thing to Pentecost imaginable. The divine presence of God was so powerfully manifested that there was no incongruity whatsoever. Men and women of all nationalities were so intent on worship that occupation with other human beings sitting near, or at a distance, did not concern them. Bidding adieu to this charming district, famous for waterfalls, and enchanting surroundings, we traveled to Hirwain (the long veldt, or common).

Hirwain had once been famous in the world for its iron industry. The contours of its roads and wide streets were eloquent testimonies of the great days gone by. The industry that had brought fame and wealth to the town had received a mortal blow by the imposition of American tariffs, the McKinley tariff more especially. Many of its prominent and respected families had been compelled to emigrate to the United States, leaving but a remnant behind. It was sad to see stark old walls standing here and there, parts of dilapidated buildings that had once provided accommodation for huge machinery to turn out thousands of tons of iron for export. Portions of railroads that were once of great service lay buried in earthmounds. A large lake, which in bygone days provided much needed water for the works, was now almost filled with weeds.

But the people were happy. New life had come. The revival seemed to have rejuvenated everybody. From tiny, spotlessly clean cottages there came music in ceaseless streams. Little organs gave forth revival hymns, while happy families sang the wonderful old hymns that were stirring Wales and the world. These family choirs attracted widespread attention, for visitors from distances commented on this characteristic of the work. Little did they know that the great choirs of our land were born in simple cottages. *Y Cor Mawr* (The Famous Choir), conducted by Caradog, which captured the world's prize in Crystal Palace in the 1870's, was made up of people who had practiced their choral pieces in humble homes in this very neighborhood. Caradog, the famous conductor, lived only three miles away, at Aberdare. Were there present in these meetings men and women who had actually sung in Crystal Palace and thereby won world-renown? It is

quite possible, even probable. These homes were ringing
with the hymns of the sanctuary, as people passed to and
fro through the streets, going to the churches where they
hoped to see and hear Mr. Roberts.

There was the generous hospitality manifested by the
people. It was not unusual to see strangers knocking at the
doors and asking if they might enter to enjoy the feast of
song provided by the family. They were welcomed.
Thrilled with the homeliness of the atmosphere and the
intense spirituality in evidence within the family circle,
what wonder that they felt a longing for its continuance?
These folk freely gave the very best that they possessed.
They gathered around their board men and women from
all parts of the world, to partake of their frugal fare,
irrespective of country, caste, or creed. Like the Maltese
of old, of whom Luke declares that they "showed us no
little kindness: for they kindled a fire, and received us
every one, because of the present rain, and because of the
cold" (Acts 28:2). There was "a fire," a spiritual fire,
kindled in Wales that dispersed "the cold" that had pre-
vailed too long in churches and homes. Consequently, they
"showed no little kindness" to all that would accept their
hospitality. Wherever revival power was felt, doors
were opened wide to welcome pilgrims, especially those
traveling long distances in pursuit of spiritual uplift. Wales
had donned her "beautiful garment" of a truth.

Hirwain being near Trecynon (the first place visited by
the revivalist outside of Loughor), what wonder that the
people walked the two miles to the meetings and literally
crowded the road! To hear them sing as they tramped
along in groups was uplifting. Scores, if not hundreds, of
them recently converted probably.

Hirwain being a junction, passengers disembarked
there for trains going in other directions. On the day the
revivalist was due, trainloads of happy people left the

station in search of the chapel where Mr. Roberts was to appear. Nobody knew to which place of worship it would be. He did go to each of them sometime during the day— I believe that he stayed only one busy day in that place.

Although Hirwain boasted very fine churches, built in the heydey of their economic prosperity, no one had dreamed that there would come a spiritual crisis in the history of the place that would tax it as the revival had done. Wherever one looked, crowds could be seen on their way to the town. Two miles over the mountain was Treherbert, at the head of the famous Rhondda Valley, well known throughout the world as the place of productive coal mines. At daybreak, one could see people going toward Hirwain. On the way they held prayer meetings on the rugged mountain. Listening to their resonant voices early in the morning created a sense of the majesty and presence of God. Five miles in another direction lay Ferndale, guarding the approaches to another Rhondda, Rhondda Fach (Little Rhondda), where the revival had been going on for weeks. Old and young came to the meetings in large numbers, utterly oblivious of the rough way over which they had to travel. They had but one purpose—to reach their destination early so as to secure a seat in one of the churches.

Wisdom suggested to the leaders that the churches should be opened early, and no sooner had keys been turned in the doors than every house of God was crowded with keenly expectant worshipers.

There was no waiting for a leader to guide the worship. That was entirely out-of-date wherever the revival had been felt in power. Every church in the place could have been filled time and again each day as the people sought admittance when Mr. Roberts was in a certain building. I was privileged to be present morning and afternoon in services where the revivalist was present. These services seemed to lack the deep spiritual tone of worship manifested in the other services when Mr. Roberts was absent. One felt that the consuming passion for seeing the leader, shown by the majority of the worshipers, militated against the freedom and anointing of the Holy Spirit experienced in several other places. Mr. Roberts spoke of heaviness and burdens. Tears ran down his cheeks almost continually. There was no agonizing outburst of weeping, yet there was a consciousness existing in our hearts that something was working against the success of that service.

Someone must have been burdened, for the hymn, "I Need Thee Every Hour," was begun during the most oppressive moments. Mr. Roberts was on his feet, for these words had stirred his spirit. Although the people sang in a subdued mood, apparently appreciative of the spiritual import of the words, Mr. Roberts lifted his long arm to signify that he wanted silence. Immediately the audience responded to his wish. Then came one of the most impressive messages that I had heard at any time. With emphasis he denounced insincerity and hypocrisy in public worship. Quietly, without an attempt at oratory, using the words of the hymn as his text, he exposed arrogant postures adopted by thoughtless people when they came to worship, as if patronizing the Almighty, especially at the time of special annual Thanksgiving for harvest. It was what might be called a "blistering" denunciation.

"Coming once in the year to give thanks for countless blessings received," said he with withering scorn that made people cringe, "brings us perilously near to blasphemy, if not to sinning against the Holy Ghost." If it is true—and it most certainly is true—that we need Him every hour, and every minute of that hour, what becomes of our boastful appearance just once a year? "Shame!" That one word dwarfed every soul that heard it. Like the crack of a pistol it rang through the building. People all over the congregation cried as though smitten with plague. When Savonarola denounced the vanity and vagaries of the flippant citizens of Florence, we are told that people by the hundreds flung themselves upon the hard pavements of the city, bewailing their sinfulness. Similar demonstrations followed immediately upon the revivalist's word in this service. God's messenger had skillfully wielded "the sword of the Spirit," and it must have drawn blood, to some extent, in every heart.

In the afternoon, the scenes of the morning were reproduced. Our revivalist spoke again on words which had been spoken in prayer, words which had evidently touched him.

> "I was not ever thus, nor prayed that Thou
>   Shouldst lead me on;
> I loved to choose and see my path; but now
>   Lead Thou me on!
> I loved the garish day, and, spite of fears,
>   Pride ruled my will. Remember not past years."

John Henry Newman's verse was repeated with such spiritual emphasis and power that everyone present must have seen strange beauty and meaning in it, some perhaps for the first time. Shortly after, a pictorial card came from the press, showing Mr. Roberts sitting at a table, writing these words which were printed underneath. This card was broadcast throughout the world as representing the thoughts of the man most prominent in the revival in Wales. One could not but feel that Newman had expressed in graphic phrase the spiritual conflicts of Mr. Roberts in the past. He was not ashamed to confess it. Were there not hundreds of others present, listening to him, who had travailed in sorrow as they remembered the "past years"? The revivalist repeated the words, "Pride ruled my will," until his hearers felt that the past were harassing him relentlessly. "Pride"!

It seemed impossible! Could this Spirit-filled vessel of the Lord have been once dominated by conceit? Was he whipping himself unnecessarily? There was certainly no trace of it at this time. We had been taught by him to pray for humbleness of spirit. Did we not hear him time and again praying the words, "Empty me! Fill me! Use me!" until they had become part of our thinking? "Remember not past years." When those words came from his lips there was no mistaking the fact that "deep was calling unto deep." It was with gladness of heart that one repeated the words, "Your sins and your iniquities will I remember no more," to himself in this tense atmosphere. "Remember not past years . . . I will remember no more." How they dovetailed in that hour of self-searching! How delightful was the recollection of the divine forgetfulness and forbearance! Mr. Roberts infused new life into the hymn that some have sung with extreme reluctance because of the galling experience through which the writer of it is reputed to have passed when they were written.

12

"THAT THEY ALL MAY BE ONE"

FOLLOWING THIS MESSAGE by the revivalist, several
voices, representing different countries, were heard in-
terceding for their beloved homeland, with China—dis-
tressed, distracted China, taking the lead. From Russia
came a cry for revival; a Baptist minister, burdened in his
spirit for his people, wept as he confessed the sins of the
nation, as Daniel did centuries ago. A German pastor sor-
rowed as he compared the greatness of days gone by, when
Luther shook the world, with his own day when his fellow
countrymen were following the vain philosophies of men.
As I review the events that have transpired since, I see
that his prayer was prophetic.

Brittany had a voice speaking to the Lord in broken
Welsh, arousing interest and enthusiasm. Some of the
words were indistinguishable while others seemed as
familiar as if the intercessor had lived in Wales for years.
He cried to the Lord for ungodly France and for his
friends enduring persecution there. A distinguished-look-
ing representative of Japan waited for a little silence, an
abatement of the fiery Welsh enthusiasm, so that he could
pray audibly. His opportunity was long in coming.

At last there came a respite, a strange, living silence.
Immediately he rose to his feet and brought Japan before
the Lord in a very definite way. At the time there was
war between Russia and Japan. In that chapel were repre-

sentatives of both nations, at perfect peace with one another, worshiping in an atmosphere that was pregnant with great possibiliᴛes for both peoples. In God's house, far away from their respective homes, there was not the slightest evidence of enmity visible between these men; both were praying for revival. They knew in their hearts that this was the only remedy for the affliction of their peoples. How they prayed! In staccato phrases and broken English, the Russian minister agonized with God. The friend from Japan, much more conversant with the Saxon language, nevertheless found it difficult to control the emotions that were in his soul. The newspapers made much of this fact next day. Russia and Japan at war in the East! Russia and Japan at peace in the West, in a small Welsh chapel!

At the same time, these newspapers were publishing statistics showing the number of professed conversions registered in the different denominations throughout Wales. Were the figures authentic? Would the exclusive Baptist church, for example, rigid in its Calvinistic theology, have considered it seemly to advertise in the secular press that so many had passed through the sacred ordinance of baptism? I think not.

A quotation from a highly reputed daily, *The South Wales Daily News,* honored throughout Wales because of its undoubted sincerity and truthfulness in its description of the revival, said: "Infidels were converted; drunkards, thieves, and gamblers saved, and many thousands reclaimed to respectability and honored citizenship. Confessions of awful sins were heard on every side, and everywhere. Old debts were remembered, and paid. Theatres and public houses in distress for lack of patronage. Several police courts had clean sheets, and were idle. In five weeks, 20,000 conversions were recorded." At a later date, the number was presumed to be no less than fifty thousand. In the eight months following the outbreak of the revival, one hundred fifty thousand had made application for church membership. However difficult it is to discover the source from which this information emanated, it would be difficult to characterize such reports as false or even fantastic. Surely the press is not usually credited with predilections favorable to the churches, or to religion in general. Their sponsoring of this marvelously spiritual movement is one of the outstanding items of this history. There is significance in the fact that they advertised the work in a manner to create world-interest so quickly.

There is before me a faded press clipping, culled, I believe, from the pages of *The Western Mail* of that time. It gives Mr. Roberts' remarks on revival, presumably delivered during the course of a service on the previous day. He is reported to have said: "You desire an outpouring of the Holy Spirit in your city? You do well. But remember, four conditions must be observed. They are *essential*.

"First, is there any sin in your past with which you have not honestly dealt,—not confessed to God? On your knees at once. Your past must be put away and cleansed.

"Second, is there anything in your life that is doubtful —anything you cannot decide whether it is good or evil? Away with it. There must not be a trace of a cloud between you and God. Have you forgiven everybody— EVERYBODY? If not, don't expect forgiveness for your sins. Better offend ten thousand friends than grieve the Spirit of God—or quench Him.

"Third, do what the Holy Spirit prompts without hesitation or fear. Obedience—prompt, implicit, unquestioning obedience, at whatever cost.

"Fourth, a public confession of Christ as personal Savior. Profession and confession are vastly different! Multitudes are guilty of long and loud profession. Confession of Christ as Lord is of recent date. We forget that there is a Trinity in the Godhead, and that the three Persons are on absolute equality. We praise the Father and we praise the Son. Can anyone produce a satisfactory reason why we should not, and do not, praise the Holy Spirit? When we speak of Him as a 'thing,' or 'something,' are we not greatly in error, since the Scriptures claim for Him absolute equality with the other sacred Persons in the Holy Trinity? Is He not ignored entirely in hundreds of the churches? Hear the word of the Lord: 'Quench not the Spirit.' That is the one way to revival. When the fire burns, it purifies. And when purified, you are fit to be used in the work of God."

Hundreds of thousands of copies of that paper entered the homes of the people each day. Try to picture what influence would be produced by such language on the minds and hearts of homely, religious folk, who were thirsting as never before for spiritual experiences. When we consider that the leading dailies, with large circulations, were sending these words into the homes of rich and poor alike, cannot this be viewed as a miracle? It was commonly reported that some of the men commissioned to follow Mr. Roberts, reporting his every word, were themselves brought under the influence of the movement and gloriously converted. Rich, powerful, influential newspaper combines do not delegate representatives to report religious movements unless they have good reasons. And what were the reasons? The people—the nation—the world clamored for news of this character. They got it "red hot." Perhaps never before, and certainly never since, have the newssheets of the world been used thus for such a high and noble purpose.

13

MERTHYR TYDVIL AND DOWLAIS

M R. ROBERTS and his helpers now visited the town of Merthyr Tydvil, in accordance with the plan mapped out for him by his secretary. The name itself is intriguing. "Merthyr" is a fine Welsh word for martyr; "Tydvil" is not so easily explained, but is reputed to be the name of the beautiful daughter of a Cymric monarch reigning among the mists and the mysteries of past centuries. Traditions have it that this lovely maiden was martyred for some mysterious reason and that this delightful title was given to the locality where she met her doom, by the fanatical loyalty of the people over whom her father reigned. They were anxious to perpetuate the name of the much loved maiden and hand down to successive generations this memorial of her deathless sacrifice. "Merthyr Tydvil," or "the martyrdom of Tydvil," thus preserves the record of a heroism thought by her contemporaries to be worthy of imperishable commemoration.

This large town had also been famous for its iron industry, which had since fallen into decay. Gaunt ruins covered its outskirts. On the hill, gazing sadly on this scene of departed industrial glory, stood the castle of the Crawshay family whose creative genius had been responsible for an organization large enough to employ hundreds of men and women. Twenty years or so previously, night skies glared with brilliance, visible twenty miles away, when the ovens of Crawshay iron works were opened and emptied. The town wore a prosperous aspect, in spite of the economic stagnation. At the time of the revival there was no evidence anywhere of poverty, except that which is found in all parts of the world where people foregather in large numbers, their crowded conditions creating physical, moral, and spiritual problems to torment municipalities and governments. People living on the fringe of things, halfway between prosperity and poverty, are always with us.

Cör Merthyr, the Merthyr Choristers, were very active at this period in the history of the town. Mr. Dan Davies had led them to many great victories. Their fame had traveled far and wide. Our National Eisteddfod platform was the scene of many a competition between the great choir conductors of Wales. Among the most famous was Dan Davies. The choristers trained by him, who obeyed implicity his baton, adored him. Invariably these famous singers were chapel or church members and every Sunday would find them in their places in the church of their choice. After the evening service they all gathered for choir practice—no sluggards permitted—until they become proficient in part-singing, so enviously proficient that they had become winners of the National Eisteddfod prize more than once.

The secret of the marvelous singing heard during the visit of Mr. Roberts to Merthyr Tydvil in those days can be attributed to this group. People thronged the main streets of the town in such numbers as to make traffic almost impossible. Backward and forward the surging throngs moved, singing revival hymns. While this manifestation of tireless energy was in progress outside the churches, similar scenes were enacted inside. Eager crowds possessed every inch of space within every place of worship in the town. Mr. Roberts seemed happy in these meetings. His demeanor always affected the congregation. When those awful spirit-burdens overwhelmed his soul, he experienced such inward agonies as to make him groan audibly. But in these meetings he appeared to be so completely at liberty in the Spirit that his buoyancy was contagious.

In one of the Merthyr meetings, a blind boy about ten years of age caused a great stir through the energy and eloquence of his prayers. A sister, not much older, had brought him many miles to the meetings. Daily he had been made acquainted with the progress of the revival through the medium of the press. Then he determined that should Mr. Roberts come within reasonable distance from his home, no sacrifice would be too great for him to make in order to be present. Sure enough, here he was, tiny hands extended in graceful gesture as he made his burning petition known at the throne of grace, while his small features radiated the very light of God. He used numerous scriptural quotations and people were astounded. Where did he acquire the vocabulary? Someone must have taken extraordinary pains to train that youthful mind to express itself so wisely, for there was no trace of childishness in his prayers. The boy had no complaints to make of the divine plan for his life. He was content to walk the dark road in sweet fellowship with his Lord.

I inquired in the churches for miles around, where I preached and conducted campaigns for years, but I utterly failed to discover a single clue that would aid in finding the lad. Had the parents moved to a distant land? No one knew. Had the little fellow died in his teens?

After Merthyr Tydvil came Dowlais. There were times, during the Dowlais visit when Mr. Roberts was almost overwhelmed with grief. Although the place was experiencing "times of refreshing," there was some obstacle preventing the operation of the Holy Spirit. With bowed head and burdened heart, Mr. Roberts spent nearly all his time in silent prayer.

The Reverend Peter Price, a popular preacher, had been pastor of the Dowlais Congregational Church for several years. His reputation as a preacher was nationwide; fearlessness characterized the messages which made an indelible impression upon the crowds of young people who listened. Many received definite blessing under his challenging denunciations of modern trends and sins. Even before Mr. Roberts started his work in Loughor, this Dowlais church was quickened under Mr. Price's ministry. It was reported that scores were joining the church. Nothing like it had been known within the memory of anyone in the district. Then came the news of the revival breaking forth in the insignificant village of Loughor, not in the large town of Dowlais. Before the unerring wisdom of the all-wise God, we bow in humble submission and, instead of questioning, we worship. As far as personal and intellectual accomplishments were concerned, there was no one in the land better qualified to guide such a movement than Mr. Price.

There was "hardness" in every service visited by the evangelist. Novices, presuming to diagnose, suggested "that the Holy Spirit had departed." Others, remembering the oft-recurring admonition to obey the Holy Spirit, suggested that He must be grieved. Very few attempted to participate in intercessory prayer.

In about half an hour after his arrival in the Congregational Chapel, Mr. Roberts arose and delivered a scathing word from the Lord. He announced that someone in that service was blocking the way of revival by criticism of the revival and, more especially, criticism of the revivalist. He declared fearlessly that the critic was not far from him and unless the spirit was expunged, he would be compelled to leave. He would not remain or take part in mock worship where the Holy Spirit was grieved. He soon departed, leaving the service to the opposition.

One morning a letter, bearing the signature of Mr. Price, appeared in the columns of *The Western Mail,* an influential daily paper. Mr. Price had attempted to correct some misconceptions, or misdemeanors, revealed in the conduct and utterances of the young converts. But the spirit of carping criticism shown toward the self-effacing revival leader, also the tendency to compare the reality of the work in his own church with that witnessed in Mr. Roberts' meetings, was extremely unfortunate. No one, surely, would ever dream of suggesting that Mr. Roberts was not engaged *unsparingly* in this glorious work, mistakes notwithstanding.

Whatever bitterness the letter might have caused in the hearts of the multitudes sympathetic to the movement, Mr. Roberts retained his composure. Studiously avoiding reference to the unpleasantness, he went on his divinely appointed mission, strong and unperturbed. "Ye have no need to fight in this battle" was the prophetic message of an age gone by, but it proved to be an up-to-date promise.

14

MR. ROBERTS GOES TO NORTH WALES

Soon after this, Mr. Roberts' sphere of service was completely changed. All over North Wales expressions were heard that he should "come over and help us." There was no evading or dismissing the call.

Now, for the benefit of those who do not know, it is well to explain that temperamentally there is a vast difference between the inhabitants of North and South Wales. Even the language, strange as it may seem, differs much in different localities. Once one leaves the region of Bible speech, it is sometimes difficult for the people to understand each other. Grammatical expressions, if strictly adhered to, make things much easier. The workaday dialect of the people can become difficult. Because of this real problem, I was obliged to refuse several invitations to conduct evangelistic campaigns in places visited by Mr. Evan Roberts in the North. Somehow one entertained a mortal dread of using a colloquialism in public speech which has different meanings in different localities. The difficulty was not an imaginary one. Who having had the experience once can deny it?

But there was and is so much in common among the Welsh people that, although geographically separated by hills, valleys and rivers, their ideals are identical . . . Politically, they have been of one mind for generations. Liberalism stood for liberty for the individual, religiously and economically. In consequence, North and South Wales stood united. Within my memory, every constituency in Wales was represented in the House of Commons by a wholehearted Liberal. Not a single delinquent among them. David Lloyd George, perhaps the greatest Welshman of our time, carried the flaming torch, and gave perfect expression to the urge inherent in the Celtic heart for liberty and independence.

Religiously, North and South Wales were of one mind —passionately religious. The chapel was the center of interest in both sections. Calvinistic Methodism predominated in the rugged North; in the more industrial South, the Baptist and Congregationalists were numerically the stronger. Each contributed its quota toward creating, in its own peculiar way, a chapel-going, Bible-loving population that made the people unique in the world. For instance, few people are aware of the fact that the British and Foreign Bible Society originated among the Welsh. The Reverend Thomas Charles of Bala suggested a Society for circulating the Scriptures in his beloved Wales, while the Reverend Thomas Hughes, a Baptist in a London pastorate, also an enthusiastic Welshman, ventured an expression of the opinion that it should include "the peoples of the whole world." Hence the adoption of the immortal slogan, well known by every Celt throughout the world, "A Bible for all the peoples of the world" *(Beibl i Bawb o Bobl y Byd)*—a sentence for its conciseness, comprehensiveness and beauty, difficult to match in any language. Thus Wales gave birth to an organization that has circulated the sacred Scriptures in the millions, and translated them into one thousand languages and dialects. What preachers different places in Wales have produced! The one-eyed Baptist preacher, Christmas Evans, was a sensational orator. Mr. Spurgeon, preaching on the text, "O! death, where is thy sting," once exclaimed, "Oh!

for the tongue of Christmas Evans when dealing with a theme like this!" John Elias O Fôn was another peerless gospel preacher, while William Williams Y Wern mightily moved his generation by his marvelous gift.

South Wales perhaps has given the largest number of revivalists and has sponsored more movements that have changed the morals of the nation. The Reverend Vavasor Powell of Radnorshire heralded the Methodist revival, his oratory shaking the whole land. The latter part of his life was spent in terrible suffering in foul prisons, but his spirit lived on. Did it kindle the flame in the heart of the Reverend Griffith Jones, of Llanddowror, leading him to establish the charity schools that assisted materially in removing the stigma of illiteracy in the Wales of his day and prepared the way for the outburst of spiritual power in the later revival? Young converts were taught to read in these simple charity schools, and this training stabilized the results of the divine movement. What shall we say of the Reverend Daniel Rowlands of Llangeitho, who, when reading the words in the Litany one Sunday morning in his church, "By Thine agony and bloody sweat," was so overwhelmed that both he and the congregation broke down? That assembly was transported in spirit to lonely Gethsemane, where they visualized the God-Man in solitary majesty and regal weakness, gripping the death-cup in His final struggle with "the despotisms, the empires, the forces that control and govern this dark world—the spiritual hosts of evil arrayed against us in the heavenly warfare" (Weymouth). It meant the beginning of a revival. Afterward came the Reverend David Morgan, Ysbutty, Pembrokeshire, in 1859, thundering his anathemas against iniquity. He moved the nation Godward as did his predecessors.

North Wales gave the godly Richard Owen to the Church, two decades or so before the period of which we are writing, a man who was consumed to ashes by the divine flame that burned in his soul. Like David Brainerd among the Indians of North America, he died a young man, mourned by multitudes, "a whole burnt-offering . . . at the door of the tabernacle of the congregation, before the Lord."

From among devotees of the revival who lived in the wealthy valleys of the South, Mr. Roberts faced the Northern itinerary, believing that God was leading him. From then on, he did not work in the South. During the progress of his mission in the North, he suffered a very serious physical collapse (of that more later) which suddenly changed the tenor of his life. Work carried on elsewhere, after this, was done by others—his brother Dan Roberts, more especially, aided by friends of his who had been blessed at the same time.

In some parts of North Wales, God's Spirit had been working powerfully for weeks, churches in some localities experiencing a quickening unknown to the present generation. Long before the advent of Mr. Roberts, they were having refreshing showers "from the presence of the Lord." The evangelist's coming, therefore, was anticipated with almost impatient keenness.

Everywhere crowds hailed him. Buildings could not possibly accommodate the multitudes that followed him. Caernarvon is noted for its fine churches. There is perhaps no city in Great Britain more richly supplied in that way. The meetings had to be held in the great Hall which provided room for ten thousand people. Even this was inadequate, hundreds being unable to find admission.

Although he was assisted wholeheartedly during his tour by the ministers of all the denominations, and there was abundant evidence that "the common people heard him gladly," there were reports trickling through, by various means and agencies, that things were not going so well with the work in the North. There was the difference in temperament of the people. Was Mr. Roberts becoming keenly conscious of this and feeling the distinction in his spirit? The Sassiwn, an annual institution dating from past generations, set apart days of preaching of the gospel when foremost preachers from North and South were invited to take part. Usually held in the open field, it was this year given over entirely to the revivalist in honor of his visit, because the majority of the people wanted it. For the moment, the voice of the finest preacher would go unheeded. Silence was golden. God was changing His method of speaking. During those days, crowds fell on their faces in the field, some seeking and crying for mercy, others noisily exuberant in a newly found Christian experience. But somehow there was a heaviness and reticence that must have seemed strange to the revivalist. Quick responsiveness and a ready spontaneity were lacking. This would be apparent only to the keenly sensitive and acutely spiritual.

Perhaps the curiosity always engendered by the presence of Mr. Roberts accounted for much of this feeling. It is possible that the Christians in North Wales had not inured themselves to the particular form that this spiritual awakening was taking. They were looking to the leader to stand on his feet, and to be like other ministers and revivalists that the older ones remembered. If so, then the difficult atmosphere, of which the revivalist must have been keenly aware, is easily explained. Had the people been brought into such a spiritual state as to forget the presence of Mr. Roberts, they would have realized the melting presence of the Holy Spirit much oftener than they did. It was a lesson difficult to learn, but when completely mastered, it led to untold blessing. The churches in the South had grasped the importance of this lesson early in the history of the mighty spiritual outbreak, for it was emphasized with such a persistency in all the meetings that the most sluggish minds could not but be impressed with its importance. When Mr. Roberts' presence was thus rigidly ignored, the spirits of the people were liberated for the purpose of worship. The heavens poured forth floods of grace into the hearts of the seeking people. Conscious of a divine anointing resting upon them, they abandoned themselves unreservedly to the power of God and experienced, in some little measure, at least, what it meant to have "power with God and with men" in intercession.

During his visit to Birkenhead and Liverpool, Mr. Roberts came into contact with this difficult spirit for the first time in his Northern tour. It probably was strange to him. There, at least, was to be found a very real cause for it. Not long after his arrival, he sensed a spirit of disunity existing among the churches, particularly in those of his own denomination. This created a bulwark athwart the pathway of the Holy Spirit, hindering His operations, frustrating the beneficent influences always emanating from His gracious presence. What would be the reaction of the Spirit-filled servant of God to such conditions? Would he ruthlessly tear aside this mask of insincerity and expose to all the world the hollowness of carnal pretenses? That is just what he did, with a courage and fearlessness that must have been God-given. But the price must have been heavy in both the physical and spiritual realm. Surrounding him on every hand were the princes and leaders of the section of the church to which he belonged, the Calvinistic Methodist Church of Wales. One can well imagine that this did not help him; it was no source of inspiration to him. Frail human nature would have immediately hoisted the flag of compromise, inscribing upon it the suggestion of a "hush-hush" policy as the wisest and easiest course. If such a thought ever came to the mind of Mr. Roberts, we have cause to render ceaseless praise to God that he was enabled by divine grace to turn a deaf ear to the seductive voice.

There was in the city of Liverpool a minister who had seceded from the denomination to which he had belonged for years. He started a church of his own, his adherents following him in large numbers out of their own denominations to associate themselves with this new work. Whether the unfortunate schism was caused by a doctrinal lapse or whether differences had risen on the question of "church government" never was clear. Disruptions of this nature in the body ecclesiastic have always brought gray hairs to young heads and unwelcome wrinkles to youthful faces of those who are profoundly concerned about the welfare of God's Zion in the world. There can be little doubt but that this outbreak in the Church of God in Wales must have caused many a heartache to the leaders.

Did Evan Roberts know of the existence of this division previous to his visit? Was he aware that the denomination to which he belonged was rent by serious schism, before he came to Liverpool? These questions arose, for the people were anxious to draw conclusions that were fair and truthful. Personally, I have not the least doubt but that the revivalist was perfectly sincere in all that he said and did at the meetings; that he would not lend an ear to local gossip. It is my unalterable conviction that Mr. Roberts spoke under the guidance of the Spirit, in obedience to a divine impulse, with the intention of rectifying the situation.

To the consternation of all present, Mr. Roberts boldly affirmed that the schismatic tendencies apparent in this movement were a definite hindrance to the working of the Spirit of God in the city, and that the persons responsible were agents of the devil. With unusual audacity, he proclaimed that a revelation had been given him to the effect that the building sedulously erected by these misguided zealots was but a house built on sand. He appealed to the people to desist and to return to their former denominational allegiance.

People today would be inclined to depreciate the importance of the declaration, concluding in their self-complacency that it was "much ado about nothing." Those fully acquainted with all the details knew only too well that there were inflammable elements inherent in the situation that could cause irreparable damage to the cause of our Lord. Mr. Roberts concluded that only a major operation, performed immediately by a skillful, steady hand, could prevent the spreading of the malady.

The conditions were serious. Things were moving to a climax. The sharp lancet of God's Word, in the form of rebuke, had to be used. To his credit be it said that he never shirked the distasteful task. Who would care to rush in, to carry out such a project, except under divine compulsion? The revivalist himself considered it important to draw his audience's attention to the existence of a potential enemy. This enemy would, unless drastically dealt with, succeed in retarding the progress of God's work in the churches, and in the revival in particular. Newspaper reports gave the subject much publicity.

Mr. Roberts' stay in those two cities was neither too long, nor too happy. Hindrances to the working of the Holy Spirit seemed to accumulate daily. It was the cause of great grief to Evan Roberts, and was symptomatic of the whole of his North Wales tour. It was widely rumored in the South that the revivalist was too much under the domination of the denomination to which he belonged; that he had, unconsciously perhaps, allowed himself to be led from the simple, unsectarian character of the previous work, and was now more partial to the large churches,

How could that be so? He arranged no meetings of his own but all were planned by the Reverend J. Mardy Davies beforehand.

————

For some time Mr. Roberts had conscientiously followed the route mapped for him. The fact that he was so completely surrounded by the leading officials of the Methodist Church may have been the cause of persistent "whispering" that Mr. Roberts was rapidly losing his personal freedom of action.

Our friends in North Wales are more reticent in regard to their religious sentiments, which fact makes them more conservative in expressing their deepest spiritual emotions. Perhaps they found it difficult, if not impossible, to liberate themselves from the bondage of their natural predilections. In which case they deserve our sympathy, instead of our censure. The people loved to hear the Word of God preached in the power of the Holy Spirit. Enthusiasm—such as they were capable of—ran high when sinners walked down from crowded galleries to make their confession of Christ. But it certainly was not the same kind of enthusiasm to be found in some other neighborhoods.

There is no doubt but that Mr. Roberts was beginning to feel that the continual strain of the work was telling upon his strong constitution. Inhaling the air of overcrowded gatherings was unhealthy. Keeping irregular hours for weeks on end without proper periods for rest was literally burning the candle at both ends. Unnumbered crowds gave him no respite, and he needed an iron constitution to survive. There was the ever present burden of souls, which could not be relinquished for five minutes. Irregular hours for sleeping; unlimited hours for working; uncontrolled hours for eating—could mortal man anywhere survive an ordeal so contrary to the laws of nature?

The first intimation that came to the public that all was not quite well was the newspaper report that he was compelled to spend a few days of rest at Capel Curig, with friends. (With the gradual prolongation of the period of rest, friends became anxious, and inquiries about his health, by telegram and letter, arrived at his address in a ceaseless stream, to the discomfort of the kind people providing the much needed hospitality.) The strain had culminated in slight paralysis of the brain, so report had it.

It was during this crisis in Mr. Roberts' life, if memory serves me aright, that Mr. and Mrs. Penn-Lewis made his acquaintance and proved such staunch friends, until they were called to be with the Lord, about twenty-seven years later.

15

THE REVIVALIST FINDS HIS CHERITH

M R. ROBERTS, like Elijah, found his Cherith.
From the moment that Mrs. Penn-Lewis came
into contact with Mr. Roberts, his life took a sudden turn.
With indications of serious indisposition appearing upon
him, drastic measures had to be taken immediately if
disaster was to be averted. Rumor circulated that already one side of the brain was paralyzed. Thousands of
willing hearts expressed readiness to come to his assistance.

At this point the Penn-Lewises come into prominence.
Impartial persons everywhere believed that these servants
of the Lord acted with the purest motive, and did so
promptly because of the urgency of the case. They urged
Mr. Roberts to take a complete rest and proffered the
hospitality of their beautiful home in Great Glen, Leices-
tershire, for the purpose.

It appears that Mr. Roberts was not enamored of the
idea at the outset, because he was not clear in his own
mind about the leading of the Holy Spirit. So, for some
days, in spite of the imminent peril to which he was exposed, he waited upon the Lord. In view of what transpired later, it was well that this had been done.

Finally, the conviction came that "the pillar of cloud"
was moving. Even then, a close friend, fully acquainted
with the details, told me that Mr. Roberts obeyed the

divine injunction with considerable diffidence. It is difficult
to account for his tardiness to "obey the heavenly vision,"
when he had always insisted on implicit obedience to every
command from the Lord. It is quite possible that the
tender Holy Spirit gave him a premonition of coming
trials.

Mrs. Penn-Lewis needs no introduction to the majority of God's children. For many years before this incident she had labored ardently in the harvest-field of
God, the heavenly Boaz. Her books, pamphlets, and ad-
dresses had provided the much needed spiritual refresh-
ment for many a fatigued, fainting laborer. She earned
the eternal gratitude of many. Unrecognized by some
Convention committees, she persisted in carrying out the
ministry entrusted to her by the Head of the Church.

That she should feel a deep interest in the young leader
of the great revival was natural, especially since that
mighty movement was in Wales. It was the country
where she had spent her girlhood days. Moreover, she had
been one of the leaders responsible for the inauguration
of another spiritual movement in Wales, the Llandrindod
Convention, for the deepening of the spiritual life of the
churches, a convention established a year or so before the
appearance of Evan Roberts. For years she had been engaged in teaching the blessedness of a higher spiritual
life provided for the Church in the death of the Lord
Jesus. This privilege procured for all believers, for all
time, she had strenuously emphasized in many parts of
the country. Her own Christian life had been completely
transformed by a gracious infilling of the Holy Spirit.
As an experienced and gifted worker for Christ, with a
wide knowledge of the mysterious working of the Holy
Spirit in the lives of God's children, she would immediately detect immaturity in the spiritual growth of the
young revivalist. Many other mature believers were con-

scious of it, but wisely winked at minor theological discrepancies which they knew were caused by inexperience. Such expressions as "He is not here; you have driven the Spirit away by your coldness" revealed limited knowledge of the work and person of the Holy Spirit. Our Lord taught, "And I will pray the Father, and he shall give you another Comforter; that he may abide with you forever . . . He dwelleth with you, and shall be in you." How, then, could He be driven away?

Further, Mrs. Penn-Lewis had witnessed incidents during this awakening that she could not approve. To her, religious enthusiasm meant that which was of the flesh, or unsanctified, unsubordinated self, the "ego" running wild. A follower of George Fox, a professed Quaker and descendant of the benevolent, tolerant William Penn, one longed to ask what was her thought of the excesses of the early Quakers who did such a wonderful work in their generation. "Fervent in Spirit, serving the Lord" was the dictum of the apostle Paul.

Mrs. Penn-Lewis must have concluded that Mr. Roberts must be delivered from this environment, in which hours, days, and sometimes nights, were spent without respite. Everybody discussed the change that was visible even in his countenance. His fine figure was bending before the storm. Is it too much now to claim for him the honor of having served a lifetime in the course of a few brief months?

So to Great Glen Mr. Roberts went, to be nursed and cared for by his generous host and hostess, in the confident hope that complete recovery would be his ultimately. But the journey to restoration was to be long and tortuous. Nevertheless, to be in the will of God—the music and the majesty of it—compensates a thousand times for discomforts. Even our *via dolorosas* are bestrewed with the fragrant flowers of God's promises, "My grace is sufficient for thee . . . My strength is made perfect in weakness." So Evan Roberts went to his beloved Cherith.

His seclusion was so complete and the watch over him so rigid that people feared and even whispered that it was against his will. His many friends concluded that such a thing could happen to a person so reduced in health as to be unable to speak for himself. Everything around him seemed to be shrouded in mystery. Letters addressed to him were unanswered. Friends from surrounding districts, including myself, called at the home in the hope of seeing the revivalist for prayer, or advice, but could not.

This created a strange situation. Rumors sped throughout Wales. This attitude was foreign to the nature of the revivalist, and acquaintances and neighbors flatly refused to believe that he was responsible. If this conduct had been dictated by a medical adviser, why had no public statement been made? When it was argued that the good friends attending to the needs of the revivalist were acting on the highest Christian principle, they were met with, "Let not your good be evil spoken of."

It is quite possible that Mr. Evan Roberts had concluded in his own mind that Mr. and Mrs. Penn-Lewis had been raised of God for this purpose, and for "such a time as this," in the history of the Welsh Revival. Had he become so spiritual in his outlook that he would not permit himself to be governed by human suggestions of any kind?

A peep behind the scenes in Island House, on the banks of the river Llwchwr would be worth while. There was the simple-hearted, warm-hearted Welsh mother, naturally proud of her world-famous son. Why should another care for him at this time of great danger? Her home was simple, but it was the only home that Evan had ever known until this time. From this happy home he had gone forth to stir the religious world. Every instinct in her mother-heart would cry out for the sacred privilege of nursing her own son.

Attempts were made to force the issue by demanding admission for the family, at least, into the home of the Penn-Lewises. But Evan Roberts was adamant. Every attempt to see him was frustrated. Admission into the house was usually comparatively easy to obtain. This must be said in fairness to the host and hostess, who must have felt keenly the difficulty of the position which they occupied. Under no circumstances would Mr. Roberts permit interference with his privacy.

Finally the Roberts family decided to make a move to clear misunderstanding. Mr. Roberts and Dan Roberts, father and brother of the revivalist, made the journey from Loughor to Great Glen, just outside the city of Leicester, in the fond hope of seeing Evan Roberts.

Their visit began well, for they were received in a spirit of Christlikeness that left nothing to be desired. Everything possible was done to make the two visitors comfortable and happy. There can be no criticism on that score. What followed is to remain a secret, evidently, for all time.

Mr. Evan Roberts maintained and defended his host and hostess. If there were any faults or mistakes, he frankly accepted all responsibility for them. All his decisions were made unaided and uninfluenced. He refused to see his father and brother. Appeals went unheeded. According to report, Mrs. Penn-Lewis made a strong effort to persuade him to discuss his situation with these members of his family, but to no avail.

Later when Dan Roberts and I stayed with mutual friends on numerous occasions, in all our conversations he exercised commendable restraint regarding his brother's conduct.

The Roberts family had been informed of the result of the Leicester visit before the return of the father and brother. Daily newspaper reports had kept them in touch with the situation. Although Mrs. Roberts idolized and idealized her son for whom the world clamored, and whom it now criticized, no word of censure was uttered by her sealed lips. Her son had brought blessing to thousands. If the mother of our Lord was aware of the angels' message, "a sword shall pierce thine heart," this little Welsh mother must suffer too.

The revival was progressing in spite of criticism. All over Wales incredible things were happening. Churches continued to enroll new members by the hundred. New voices were heard assisting in the progress of the work. There was no lack of evidence regarding the reality of the mighty outpouring. Statistics appeared in the columns of the daily newspapers announcing considerable improvement in the attendance of miners and others employed. Because of this fact, output in factories, coal mines, iron and steel works, spiraled upward unbelievably.

Of the results consequent upon the outbreak of the revival the most marvelous was the effect upon the courts of justice throughout Wales. In several towns, especially those of the seaports and mining districts, judges and magistrates commented upon the effect produced by this movement upon proceedings in their courts. Criminal calendars were reduced to a minimum. Prison wardens must have imagined that something approximating the Millennium, if not the thing itself, had happened. Twirling thumbs, instead of rattling ponderous keys, was a strange experience for them. Lists of convictions dwindled to nothing. Judges had, instead of the usual long lists of cases awaiting trial, blank sheets of paper, without a single name.

To celebrate the auspicious occasion, pairs of snow-white gloves were ceremoniously handed to them, to be preserved scrupulously as a witness to future generations of the reality and blessedness of real revival. This ancient custom, so rarely performed or witnessed, had persisted within the British Isles since the birth of the legal code. For that generation to have had the honor of gazing upon such a ceremony was a privilege that would be coveted by the people of any civilized country. But the vast majority of unthinking people allowed the unusual happening to pass without lifting an eyebrow. Such indolence—who can understand or explain it? What would the nations of the world give today to witness such a sight? Courts are overcrowded, criminal sheets are lengthening daily, law-breaking is fashionable with the multitudes. Legal authorities are overwhelmed by the number of intricate problems, and sacred matrimonial bonds are held so loosely that their dissolution becomes a matter of little, if any, concern. After over forty years, one is constrained to declare that those revival times were wonderful days in which to live. Would to God, in view of the perilous days in which we live and the imminent return of our Lord, that a reproduction of those times could be witnessed, so that the countless thousands around us might be gathered in before it is too late, and the door forever shut!

With the passage of time and the removal of Evan Roberts, other men of God, representing all the denominations in Wales, were called and equipped to carry on the work. Gradually, the great fervor began to die down and the time arrived for constructive work, the edification and building up of the young converts. They were becoming more amenable, more ready to sit down in quietness to listen to the exposition of the sacred Scripture by men endowed with power by the Holy Ghost. Mr. Dan Roberts, although subdued in spirit, continued to carry on his brother's work. He traveled constantly up and down the country, endeavoring to keep revival flame burning. In the Congregational denomination, Keri Evans rendered Trojan service in his capacity as teacher and expositor. His logical mind, reinforced by a dynamic Christian experience, made him an outstanding advocate of the principles undergirding the revival. All that he possessed was placed unreservedly at the disposal of the Holy Spirit. Dr. H. Elvet Lewis, Kings Cross, London, used his great gifts and mighty influence in the same direction, to the building up of the faith of the young converts.

No one can fail to mention the name of David Evans of Bridgend. With unflagging zeal he pursued the course mapped out for him by the Head of the Church.

The ministry of the Word was restored to its place of eminence among the converts. The period of unconventionality had expired. In all the revival meetings for which David Evans was humanly responsible, he quietly insisted upon delivering his message. Sometimes, and it happened frequently, he was interrupted by an outburst of fervor; at such times, he remained calm until the enthusiasm ceased. For many years, evangelical and especially evangelistic ministers possessing the revival touch had to be prepared for these interruptions.

The Llandrindod Convention, or, as some preferred to call it, the Welsh Keswick, had its inauguration at this time. God is never behind time in His bounteous provision for His Church. In 1903, before the outbreak of the revival, the Convention's first meetings were held in the delightful surroundings of the famous health resort. Enthusiastic adherents of the tenets of the Keswick convention felt led to extend the influence of those great gatherings to Wales. They had experienced an urge to establish a work in Wales that would be typically Welsh in temperament. Among the foremost leaders were such men as Canon Talbot Rice, A. T. Pierson and F. B. Meyer.

16

REVIVAL REPERCUSSIONS

THIS STORY would be incomplete without some reference to the abiding results of such a wonderful outpouring of the Holy Spirit—one of the most spontaneous and instantaneous in the annals of the Church of God. It is doubtful whether historians can refer to another such illustration of the majesty and sovereignty of the Godhead. To all the younger elements in the Church at that time the revelation was both startling and stupendous. That God in His infinite wisdom should have chosen the little nation of Wales for the manifestation of such unprecedented power was, and still is, humbling. We admit that the honor conferred upon us was undeserved.

However, there are elements lying dormant in the Celtic nature which, when sanctified and impregnated by a mighty baptism of the Holy Spirit, can produce mighty effects upon the minds and consciences of others. Also, under the stirring ministries of Christmas Evans and John Elias, followed by many others of a later period, thousands of their contemporaries were revolutionized in their moral lives. Like all previous similar manifestations, the 1904-5 outpouring left unmistakable impressions, although it might have differed in character from other movements.

Orthodox theology has always proved to be the hidden source of true revival. Men have stumbled accidentally over some portion of Scripture which has subsequently proved to have resident within itself the germ of eternal life. They have dared to believe it to be the very Word of God, the divine Logos that produces a new nature whenever and wherever it is relied upon. The written Word suddenly becomes the living Word. Heart-belief turns to heart-experience. In the strength and buoyancy of this new experience individuals have gone forth into a world submerged in sin to proclaim a message that has completely changed their own lives and the lives of all who believe it with the heart.

Nothing worthwhile has ever happened in the history of the Church since Pentecost but what is based upon an unshakable belief in the power of the eternal Word. When we think of Augustine, every unbiased mind must confess that when he heard the voice in the solitudes of the garden saying, "Take up the book, and read," and his eyes rested on the words, "Put ye on the Lord Jesus Christ," it was a glorious day for the inert Christian Church. Her greatest teacher for fourteen centuries was "born again" that very moment. When the eternal city, so described by every one of her proud citizens, was crumbling and falling to fragments, a vision of the City of God was granted this peerless servant of Christ, the proclaiming of which produced a steadying effect upon the minds of distracted mankind everywhere.

Luther was granted a similar experience when, on an eventful occasion as he climbed the Santa Scala, accompanied by scores of other soul-weary pilgrims, seeking succor from the taunts of an awakened conscience, he heard a voice uttering the words, "The just shall live by faith." Rising rapidly from his servile position, he was now confronted with a new world, never again to bow the knee in the House of Rimmon. His great soul, torn by many a fierce tempest, now entered a heaven of perfect

tranquillity. Has there ever been among the giants of the
faith a greater than he? Like Saul of Israel he towered
above his brethren. One brief sentence of only six words
proved the sacred Scriptures to be "like a fire, and like a
hammer that breaketh the rock into pieces." On All
Saints' Day—surely a significant date—in 1517, Luther
nailed his ninety-five theses on the church door.

Next the name of John Wesley appears. The historian
Lecky unhesitatingly pronounced the conversion of this
man to be "an epoch" in British history. Did it not result
in the emancipation of the British Isles from the impending horror of a dominant, Godless materialism that was
ravaging the soul of emotional France at the time? The
magnitude of such an occurrence stands out conspicuously
at the present time in human affairs. We see the Russian
colossus with its atheistic philosophy overspreading the
frontiers of nations unable to defend their democratic
heritage. Listen to Wesley's personal testimony in his
Journal:

> "In the evening, very unwillingly, I went to a Society in
> Aldersgate street where one was reading Luther's preface to
> the Epistle to the Romans. About a quarter past nine, while
> Luther was describing the change which God works in the
> heart through faith in Christ, I felt my heart strangely
> warmed. I felt I did, at that moment, trust in Christ alone
> for salvation. And an assurance was given me on the spot
> that He had taken away my sins, even mine, and had thus
> saved me from the law of sin and death."

Thus Wesley entered into the succession of triumphant
reformers, originating with the apostle Paul and preserved
through the instrumentality of Athanasius and others, all
of whom affirmed their unshakable faith in the imperishable Scriptures of truth.

Evan Roberts enters the same catagory. He believed
emphatically and proclaimed fearlessly his faith in the
inerrancy and inviolability of God's holy Word. All his
service and action were based upon this elevated concep-

tion of divine truth. The Bible had been his inseparable companion since early childhood days. To see his illumined countenance, as he lovingly waved aloft his precious Bible in the course of some meetings, was a real tonic to any despondent soul. At the time of my writing, he has passed the three-score years and ten. Since 1906 he has studiously refrained from participating actively in public life. Occasionally he would present himself in an unofficial capacity, at some of the high religious festivals prominent in Welsh religious life. Often his unobtrusive presence would pass entirely unobserved. His collaboration with Mrs. Penn-Lewis in producing the book, *War on the Saints,* was a gratuitous denial of the reality of much of the finest work done by the revival while it proceeded on its irresistible course. How anyone who had witnessed the miracles of grace wrought during this wonderful manifestation could possibly ascribe so much of it to Satanic influences poses a conundrum. Is there any human being in existence anywhere who would foolishly deny the possibility of unpleasant occurrences during revival time? Such periods represent the abnormal in the experience of the Church of God.

In discussing some of the results remaining as permanent memories of this marvelous Wales revival, one naturally thinks of those servants of Christ who were brought into a definite experience of the saving grace of our Lord, or were brought to a place of self-surrender resulting in a fullness of the Holy Spirit leading them out into wider and greater spheres of service for their Master at this time. A much longer narrative than is intended in these pages would be necessary if all the cases known to us were tabulated. Let it suffice here if but a few of them are mentioned.

The far-famed name of Stephen Jeffries, later Pastor Jeffries, leaps to memory. His evangelistic exploits throughout the length and breadth of the British Isles remain a treasured memory. He was born and "born again" in the mining village of Nantyffyllon, South Wales.

John Thomas, brilliant scholar and peerless preacher, was in his youthful days a pit boy in Wales. A serious accident, causing lifelong physical deformity, filled his mind with serious thoughts for the future that ultimately led him to prepare for the ministry. After spending many years in the ministry, notably in Liverpool, Mr. Thomas relinquished all pastoral responsibilities to pursue a free-lance program. What a boon this was to Wales, just at the time when such a man was needed to encourage the thousands of young converts who were crying for "the bread of life"! The way opened for the great preacher to visit colleges, churches, even mission halls, ministering to the crying needs of young believers everywhere.

Another firebrand, Pastor Jenkins, converted when "the fire fell" in Cross Hands, Carmarthen, Wales, has held successive pastorates on The Rand, Transvaal, South Africa, with manifest success and appreciation. This is proved by the fact that he held this honored position in one church for over twenty years—no mean attainment for a man who could not boast of academical training. He went straight from the pit to the pulpit.

John Daniel Jones, familiarly known far and wide as John Dan, had run in the swift race in the prodigal way for years. His conversion in the revival was a "right-about-face" business, and no one could question it. The work of grace in his heart made him a delightful companion. At the time of his conversion his reading was very defective. Between the words and sentences there were prolonged halts and painful stammerings. This was marvelously rectified in a very brief time. Soon it became a delightsome experience to listen to him reading the Scriptures in public.

In a simple cottage meeting, with about two dozen persons present, just when the fervency of the revival was gradually and visibly waning, another soul surrendered to the claims of the Lord for work in India. John Evans not only submitted himself, which meant much, but he also surrendered the careful savings of many years, which must have meant a considerable sacrifice, if such a word should be used in this sacred connection. The year 1908 saw him enter his training, medical and otherwise, before departure for India, the sphere of his lifework. Every report received indicates that his service in the vineyard of the Lord has been greatly blessed. We have mentioned only a few, each a "brand plucked out of the fire." Thus were revival influences spread to all the world.